In memory of...

Martine Vallée

The winds of time blow constantly … unceasingly. Sometimes they bring wonder and sweetness, and sometimes the winds of time are harsh. It is the test of the Old Soul to work with both, and to bend accordingly in this wind, without breaking.

Sometimes this is easier said than done.

Martine Vallée was an incredible, bright light for myself and so many others. She and her brother, Marc, became our French Canadian door to the world. They were the ones who, for over twenty years, translated and published the wisdom of Kryon in the French language for each of the Kryon books. As an original partner in Ariane Publishing, Martine was also instrumental in pulling me out of my shell, to travel to France for my first ever trip to Europe.

Her departure from this world in September 2015 was a blow. Young, vivacious, and ultimately caring about everything, she was a force for the integrity of everything good on this planet. Then she was gone.

These are the times when we ask "Why?" and when we shake our heads, trying to understand the esoteric plans of Spirit. For us, it is inappropriate, and sorrowful. She did so much, and was not finished!

Kryon tells us that, "We don't know what we don't know." I accept this, and look forward to discovering the hidden gift that is always promised. But in the meantime, she is greatly missed every passing day.

Thank you Martine, for enriching my life so much.

Lee Carroll

THE NEW HUMAN
The Evolution of Humanity
Kryon Book 14

Publisher: **The Kryon Writings, Inc.**

P.O. Box 28871
San Diego
California 92198

Kryon books can be purchased in retail stores,
by phone or on the Internet at [www.kryon.com/store].
(800) 352-6657 - E-mail <kryonbooks@kryon.com>

Written by Lee Carroll, Ph.D (hon)

Cover Design by Deborah DeLisi

Primary Editing by Lourana Howard

Additional Editing by Dawne Brooks

ISBN# 978-188805320-3 $16.95

THE NEW HUMAN
The Evolution of Humanity

Kryon
Book 14

NEW

Original, fresh, imaginative, creative, contemporary, up to date, futuristic.

NEW HUMAN

Compassionate, humane, kind, considerate, understanding, sympathetic, tolerant, approachable, accessible.

Table of Contents

Introduction

Lee Carroll

Kryon
Book 14

Introduction

Greetings, I am Lee Carroll. Welcome to KRYON book fourteen!

Well, it actually may not be book fourteen, since I have lost track of how to count KRYON books! Some years ago, many of the foreign language publishers took advantage of the channellings and the Q&A section of the KRYON website, and made other KRYON books out of them, using other numbering protocols. In addition, the last three years have spawned three more KRYON books, which have been compilations of the KRYON channellings over 26 years. So, I guess I should say, "Welcome to another KRYON book"!

This is normally where I explain KRYON, as if you didn't know, and warn you that strange channellings are coming. But not this time. This is my twenty-sixth year, and if you are actually reading this, then you already are aware of this beautiful, loving energy called KRYON. If you picked up this book by accident ... Laugh out loud! There are no accidents. Keep reading.

KRYON book thirteen was released at the beginning of 2013, and was presented just after the 2012 "marker." KRYON called this transition a marker, because it was the turning-point that determined if humanity was going to stay or not. The book was called *The Recalibration of Humanity.* A massive change was about to occur, and the Ancients had predicted it. KRYON was here because of it, and the entire book outlined how all this had happened, and revealed profound information of the ages that backed it up. It wasn't KRYON information – it was sacred history, and had been the prophesy of original humanity for centuries. I would invite you to read this book if you want a full picture of what has begun on this planet, and the surrounding channellings that took place right before the shift began. [www.kryon.com/store]

Here we are some years later, and now we are starting to see differences and feel some changes. For many, this shifting reality comes with fear, misunderstanding, and uncertainty. For most, any change is uncomfortable. This means that the "waiting for the other shoe to drop" syndrome is alive and well, and humanity is slowly moving into an era that has no guideposts of normalcy. We now sit in a major shift, and are being pushed and pulled in many directions, as we start to evolve spiritually.

In order to really give you the core of what this book is about, I'm going to reveal to you something that happened to me, that has been a secret in my life for years.

DECEMBER 21, 2012 –

Sometimes Akashic remembrance can play tricks on you. It can scramble who you are and where you are, and change reality itself. Normally, it does this during dreams; however, if you are one who has given permission and intent for your past life experiences to come forward to your *now*, reality itself can temporarily shift. Sometimes this can happen, even if you didn't actually think you gave intent, but instead, you started becoming interested in esoteric things, and studied energies that were new to you. Did you ever have a "brain scrambling experience" perhaps, or find yourself with a sudden change in your life that you didn't expect? Shhhh ... you didn't think I knew that, huh? Never tell anybody if this happens to you. That's what makes psychiatric services so crowded. So of course, this is our secret – reality-shifting Akashic episodes! But it's actually more common than you think, among Old Souls.

It may only be in movies that you have seen this, where the music gets serene and soft, and the sonorities of the tones seem to target the "change" about to happen to one of the main characters. Sometimes the screen will be oversaturated with white, and the image will dim into the pixels of brilliance and objects will have slight halos around them. It's film magic that says "get ready for the unreal." However, with me there was no movie – and no music – or was there?

I was in Hawaii, which is my heart's center-point on the planet. It was morning and I was casually walking to a place where 900 people would eventually meet, sing, celebrate, and welcome-in a new era on Earth. It was a major metaphysical meeting, with Dr. Todd Ovokaitys and the Pineal Toning "choir." I would channel many times throughout the Toning event all day, and I knew it was going to be important, elegant, energetic, and profound. But as I passed a place that overlooked the ocean, suddenly I wasn't really there at all.

It was a typical beautiful day in Maui, and a gentle warm wind was blowing in from the ocean. It was like the very breath of Mother Nature – Gaia – as she gently caressed the air to provide a benign and benevolent breeze that could soothe anyone in its path. I could hear the eternal, unending sound of the surf, and it started to sing within my Akash – that place in the DNA where every memory of every lifetime is stored. I pondered how those who lived here ages ago had enjoyed the same sound as I was enjoying right now, but somehow, it blended with this moment – I was slowly slipping into a haze of my past. I was *here* and *there*, at the same time. This constant, pounding surf had been breaking and turning over on itself for eons, right here where I was. It was an awesome, powerful force that contained the secrets of all history. It had seen everything, and had endured war and storm, and the very dispensation of the ages of Earth itself, and it never stopped.

The emotional release of a warm wind on your face within a stellar ocean setting doesn't change much over the millennia, at least the feeling you get from it. It somehow carries with it a tincture of moisture from the surf on your face and in your hair, and suddenly, you are part of everything that ever happened there. Sometimes you don't even want to breathe, for fear it will stop the vision, and other times, you want to take it all in, and you may take the biggest cleansing breath you can. You close your eyes and lift your head in the direction of the sound of the surf – that sound that never stops – and no matter who is with you – you are alone for that moment.

This experience of nature speaks to you in ways that are beyond any known Earth language, if you let it. It can capture you like the siren songs that seafarers have known about forever. It can transport you to places that are only known by the history of the sand beneath your feet. I was aware that, even thousands of years ago, the sound of the waves and the wind on your face on a warm day could stop you in your tracks. It's almost as if you heard *your own music,* and the elements seemed to be speaking to you. What were they saying to me today? Was it just wind, or was there another language trying to get through? Perhaps these pristine elements were asking me if I would join them just for a moment? Perhaps they were saying, *"I know you! – I know you!"*?

Suddenly, my dress shoes were gone and I was barefoot. My skin was a different color, even though I had no way to verify it. My hair was thick and long. Sometimes you just "know" who you are, like in a dream where you are transported to another place and you are another person entirely. I knew I had been here, or at least on this island in some way that was not logical or measurable with anything that I could understand. Was I channelling? The feeling was similar, and I half-expected that I would be taken to that magic place where I could actually see the light of creation and hear the music of the other side of the veil. But not this time.

I don't know how much time passed, but I stopped and faced the ocean. I became slightly dizzy, which isn't uncommon these days, but it was then. I hung on to a convenient post that was oddly unfinished and rough-hewn. I was aware of this, and didn't want to get splinters, because the salt water would sting when I entered the water. What? I wasn't going into the water! What was happening? Was I having an "Akashic moment" or was there more?

This wasn't the first time I've had this happen to me in Hawaii. But it was the first time that it almost "took over" and carried me with it. I kept my eyes open, since a take-over wasn't something I wanted at this moment. I hoped that by keeping my eyes open, it would keep me in my present reality and help with the dizziness, but at last, I closed my eyes. I had to. The *music* of the surf was too intense, and the feeling of peaceful serenity was too alluring.

Mom was there, but it wasn't really Mom. It was her voice, a voice I hadn't actually heard since her departure forty years earlier. But then it changed and wasn't my Mom at all. It was my "original mom." The voice was feminine, but the countenance was divine. Perhaps it was Mother Nature, or even Pele? After all, I was in Hawaii! But a message was given, and I have saved it until now. Even those closest to me have never heard this story, as I will explain. It was just too personal, and I weep when I try to tell it to anyone. I knew I was under some pressure, with what I was going to begin doing in a few hours, so I was ready to have something sweet and peaceful become mine for a moment in time. What was the message? It was something so cryptic that I couldn't put it together. Did you ever have a dream, and you woke up, but when you tried to talk about it, it was nonsense? That was the case, until now. Until this book.

I don't get messages with linear auditory voices. I never did. I "hear KRYON" through visions and thought packages. It's difficult to explain, but I have been doing this for so long, that it's absolutely normal to me. It's a language of its own, like an ongoing intuition that stays put, so that I can perceive it, and it's very multidimensional. To many, it would seem to be "all over the place," but to me, it makes sense, and I interpret all this in a straight, linear, logical line called Human speech. It's something I had to learn to do, and those who heard me in the early days know that I sweated with it so hard that I often had to change shirts during breaks between channelling segments. That was long ago.

I got the vision, and it wasn't what I thought it would be. I was fully expecting what I had seen before – a revelation of my role as a runner on Maui to the top of the mountain to the Temple of Rejuvenation. This was a common image, and very real to me. But what came next was different – really different: It was me in the ancient past – again, and me in the now, but then something was odd and strange. The motherly voice was droning in the background, but the words were not clear. Instead, I got pictures – and they were all over the place.

My body was old, but not old. It had years on it, but not age. How do I explain this? Suddenly, I was a "future Ancient," and that made no sense. I guess if you measure age in "Moses years," then it's not really relative to our own perception of age. I was in a young body with lots of years on it. It was measured in centuries! I felt that all the experiences of my Akash were within me, alive on the Earth. I felt so empowered that I could almost fly, and I absolutely knew it. The motherly voice droned on, and I didn't hear any of it clearly. I realized that this voice was simply the *bed of energy* within which this vision needed to exist. My wisdom was so great, I could write volumes of books about almost anything! I had control over my health and how I aged, and physics was mine. I knew it all, and felt I could control it.

In my mind, and at that time, there was only one explanation: I had been an Ascended Master on the planet! Now I understand the real interpretation, and feel so foolish at my lack of perceptive understanding. But now you know why I never talked about this.

All these years, I felt it was an "ego" vision, completely and totally manufactured by that part of me which I try to suppress in my life. I was never going to tell anyone that I had a vision of being a reincarnated Ascended Master! That would be the worst thing I could think of for anyone to hear, and would put me squarely in the same category as all those Gurus who want to charge you money to forgive your sins, or have you sit at their feet for $5,000 an hour while you contemplated your navel (or theirs). But now I know what this message was really about. Finally, I now more fully understand what had happened that day.

The Akashic Record of your body is multidimensional. Although we feel it is linear, and like some kind of history book, it is not. It deals with, and remembers, the *energy* of lifetimes of emotion, compassion, and lessons. But that's not all. It projects, too. In a multidimensional state, there really is no linear time, as we know it. It's *time in a circle,* with potentials of repeating energy. A circle never ends, and time never ends. There is no beginning or end to a circle. So, does that mean that our future is contained in that closed circle? How could that be, since we create our own future as we go, and events haven't happened yet? The answer is one that is difficult, if not impossible, to teach. Think of it this way: In the circle, an infinite amount of possibilities are already there for an infinite amount of time – all possibilities. As we create things, we activate certain possibilities that are already there as potentials waiting to be activated. But in the process of activating something new, we also create the activation of a bunch of other possibilities to come, which naturally are related to it.

I borrow from Bruce Lipton and Gregg Braden when they talk about how the string of a guitar will harmonically vibrate, if a frequency close to it is loud enough, and is the same frequency or note in music. So, without being touched, a string can vibrate at a resonant vibration, as the other string is sounding close to it. Time is similar, and if you create something profound, such as a world-changing invention, it creates resonant vibrations with potentials of the future, now that the invention exists. Those resonances are not predictions or prophesies, but rather, they are simply resonating things on the circle of time to come. Confused? Okay, here is a metaphor for you:

Think of it this way: In baseball, pretend you have a championship game, it's a tied score, and you have a man on third base. In this pretend scenario, this could be the "winning run" of the game, and it's a setup for the future. All the fans resonate to the setup of winning, and they are anxious and cheering. What happens next is not guaranteed, and many things could change it. But having the man on third is a strong potential of a victory. So if someone says, *"I think we will win!"* Is that telling the future? Is it wishful thinking, or is it sensing the energy of the potential that is there? Having the man on third is resonating to a coming potential of a victory – in the future.

Passing the marker of 2012 was more than just a time when we went past a critical point in our history. It was a set-up for the future, and everything started to resonate in that multidimensional circle of time. According to quantum physicists, this is the paradigm of the way time really works. Time is also variable with speed, gravity, and who knows what else at this point. We are discovering new things about our reality with each passing year.

In Maui, I wasn't being shown who I was in the past, I was receiving a message of what was coming! I completely missed it, and now I get chills to think of what the real message was. This was the NEW HUMAN! We were starting a DNA evolvement, and would eventually become masters of age, health, physics, and our own reality. This was going to become a planet in "Ascension status," something that KRYON has talked about since his arrival in 1989. It was a prediction!

The post I had been hanging onto became fine polished marble, as built by the hotel. My dress shoes were back on, and I stood there mystified. I was also a bit aggravated, since my hair was now mussed up from the wind – I was always trying to keep my very thin hair under control. Now I *really* knew I was back to reality. My odd and curious mind wondered if Masters had better hair.

Why did I get that amazing message? Ego-driven self-importance is equivalent to a spiritual death sentence in all my teaching. KRYON says it stops growth and takes you in odd directions. Often, it is self-destructive. I've seen it within my own professional circles! So why did I get a message that seemed to put me on a pedestal? It's because I wasn't ready to understand it, and now I do.

As the KRYON channel, I now feel like a rank beginner to have missed this totally logical message. It was very logical that I would receive this message, with what I was about to do: I was about to participate in the celebration of passing this very important marker for humanity, which would then set up ripples in time, like the winning run in baseball! I knew what it meant, since the potentials of it had been channelled over and over. So, on my way to the event, KRYON was trying to give me a stellar and profound message of what we all could eventually achieve. He was showing me a Human who would be totally different than we could ever conceive. What did I do with this elegant message? I suppressed it as an ego message, and I never let it out. Now I write a book about it.

Humanity is on the edge of a major consciousness shift. It will take a long, long time, but time is guaranteed and abundant (according to KRYON). Time goes by, and we learn and grow. But now our paths will be different, and that's what this book is about, for channel after channel, KRYON has given some of the potentials that are coming our way, as we evolve into a new consciousness for the planet. Now you know why it is called "The New Human." It's the long overdue evolution of the consciousness of humanity.

Oh, by the way, I asked KRYON if I would have better hair next time. The answer sounded like it came from my own brain. Okay, it did. Sometimes I feel I have some kind of really inappropriate comic Tourette's Syndrome, and things just fly out of my brain unchecked.

"Hair today, gone tomorrow," was the answer. Next time, I'll probably have no hair.

The Metaphor of the Playground

All through the channellings of this book, there are references to "getting out of the playground." This is a constant metaphor that KRYON has used, and I wish to explain it. It makes total sense, if you think about it.

If one hundred percent represents mastery, for eons our consciousness has been working at about thirty percent. We call it "Human Nature," but it's really a consciousness of dysfunction. We are built to be so much more efficient in so many things, including how we age and the very efficiency of our DNA, but we are stuck in the low thirty percentages.

Real proof of this, is the history of humanity. We never evolved. Oh, we got new toys and inventions, but we never evolved. We have been in basic survival mode since the beginning, and only now are we starting to climb out of it. We started killing each other for resources and power, or the whims of the Royal few, right from the start of history. We gave each other the horror and sorrow of war, and the death and suffering of millions. Then we did it again and again and again. It's almost like we never learned that it just didn't work! One war led to another, and often, it was the same war, with the same players, in a serial fashion.

Throughout history, great philosophers have given us many aphorisms that basically say, it is the fool who tries the same thing over and over, expecting different results. We are the fools. Over and over, war created more war.

It was almost like countries existed to produce conquering armies and navies, and if you look at the major countries of Earth, they ALL did it! We are a warring society, and the sad part of it is, that we still expect to be. The "ripples" of time say we are "overdue" for another war! It's so ingrained in us, that it has become normal for humanity. We are actually expecting the next installment of our dysfunction.... Until now.

I'm not going to review what happened to change all this. That was done in KRYON Book 13, "*The Recalibration of Humanity.*" The Ancients actually predicted that if we got beyond the expected Armageddon of the year 2000, and passed the precession of the equinoxes of 2012, we would begin to have the potential of higher consciousness. This prophesy was written in their calendars, etched into the walls of their buildings, and scratched into the rocks of the mountains where they lived. It was everywhere!

The definition of higher consciousness is a consciousness that would begin to work together in compromise and cooperation, to make society function without war. *No more war* would be a "given" and not the end-all, or main goal. It would be the beginning of a new world, and new thinking. KRYON has even predicted that eventually, historians would look at history and call everything before 2012, "The barbarian era." There is even a chance that we might again designate time from this point, just as we did with BC and AD – representing a profound event that changed the energy of the planet. Only time will tell, but meanwhile we are in transition – a great shift.

I ask you, Old Soul, who wants war? In an energy of "no more fence-sitting" (as KRYON has said), you can see who wants it. The lowest and most basic survival consciousness on the planet is still doing it, but now we all get to see the differences in thinking, and the "black and white hats" are getting more obvious to all humanity. It's almost that delineated right now, on our evening news. There are now armies without borders or even a common language, who simply want to destroy peace, kill anyone who is around, behead family members on TV, and create havoc in public places with bombs that tear apart bodies. This kind of terrorism is new, never before organized in this way. These are new times, in which the darkness on this planet is raging against the new enhanced light starting to develop in the millions of awakening Old Souls everywhere. The dark is losing strength, and they know it.

Most of you reading this have children. In fact, we all were children at one time. Do you remember what happened at school on the playground when you were about eight years old? Your psyche wasn't developed yet. Most children are just discovering how social interaction works with non-family members. Self-worth is an elusive and graduate concept, not yet developed in most eight year olds.

The result is a microcosm of how humanity works. Many choose their friends carefully, and "circle the wagons" against other groups of kids from another sex, race, religion or neighborhood. Then there are the bullies, rock-throwers, or verbally abusive kids, who seem to gain power from calling names or being unkind about clothing or looks in general. It goes on and on. This is where children come home over and over in tears about who did what to whom, and it's sorrowful and difficult for them. Then there are the trips to the principal's office of the school to discipline or mediate hurtful situations. At that age, we were all simply pushing the envelope of growing up. Some were faster than others at learning how to take advantage of their peers' weaknesses, and often took control. Sound familiar?

Now, turn the page. Your children are eighteen. It's only ten years later and suddenly, everything has changed. There is a greater maturity of self-awareness, and now these young adults are more comfortable with others. They are involved with social media (or whatever was the rage of social meeting places in the past). They have cars and are more secure with their own abilities. They come and go freely, and they are interested in each other, the hobbies and clothing, and who is doing what. They are no longer isolated and surviving in anxiety, fearing the unknown – they have matured, and some are even finding an elegance in their relationships that is rewarding. Some bullies are still there, but they have isolated themselves into groups of other bullies. The mold is set for everyone on their ideas of how to "get along with others." High school and universities are *play time*, and are often memorably the finest years of a young person's life. Only ten years, and so much has changed!

KRYON says that this is the metaphor of what is happening on the planet. We never grew up, and have been stuck in the playground of consciousness. We have done it for so long that we just assume that *Human Nature* is this way, and often assign that term to a negative attribute of behavior. We never experienced anything else, so there *is* nothing else. But what if there were?

When you are eight, it's a complex and difficult world of unknowns, and the concept that it will all clear up some day is simply not there. KRYON has a saying that has been used over and over through the years: "You don't know, what you don't know." It's simply a way of saying that you can't think beyond your existing knowledge, to a higher knowledge that you have not experienced yet. So humanity in general has no idea of what is coming, or how thinking may change. For that matter, how everything may change.

This book makes an assumption that we are coming out of the playground, and the channellings begin to tell us what might be next. This is all based on what we have already started to see: Enter the Indigo Children.

The Indigo Children Revisited

Over fifteen year ago, Jan Tober and I wrote a simple little book called "*The Indigo Children*." The title was based on an observation by a woman named Nancy Tappe, who "saw" a new indigo color around recently born children. Nancy had a form of synesthesia, in which her enhanced brain function would see energy as colors and shapes. With her permission, we introduced the concept that children with these new colors (indigo was one) represented children of new consciousness being born on the planet.

The book that Jan and I wrote was the best-selling book at Hay House for that year. Who knew? It went mainstream! Why? Because millions of parents all over the planet were seeing it, relating to it, and it was causing major behavior issues that started the whole industry around ADD and ADHD. The kids were changing, and our book was the first one to publicly give it a name and identify what was going on. These children were pre-cursors of a difference consciousness, and we pegged it.

"*But wait,*" some of you say. "*How can that be? We hadn't passed that 2012 marker yet. Many of them actually were coming in during the Cold War during the sixties, seventies, and eighties!*" The answer is now easy to explain. Read the above explanation in this chapter about the potentials of time. These different consciousness kids were "*The potential winning run on third base.*" They represented a potential future of what was coming for us all. Again, this is the way time works, and although it may be confusing to you, it has been seen in history over and over. Did you ever wonder why our major inventions, including the telephone and powered flight, all seemed to occur at the same time on the planet? Often, one inventor beat out others by only a week, or even hours? It was so close with the invention of radio broadcasting, that there is still controversy about who did it first! It seemed like new, revolutionary ideas were somehow presenting themselves at the exact same time all over the planet. That's the "ripple effect" of potentials that we are speaking of.

The Indigo Children were not difficult, but different. They had far more self-worth at an earlier age. This made them seen headstrong, but they simply knew more about how things work, and systems dealing with an older energy were not working for them. What made that difficult for parents and society was they acted out when they were put into dysfunctional systems (such as current school education and old linear parenting practices). I invite you to find and read this book. Actually, there are now three Indigo books by Jan Tober and myself.

The most recent Indigo book is my favorite, because industry and education was starting to see it, and react. I loved the reports from major fast-food chains, whose managers were pulling out their hair and asking, *"What's wrong with the young people today?"* It seems that first-job positions, usually working in the back room of hamburger production, were in trouble. These young people, being trained to go from step A to B to C to D, were universally rebelling. They would say, *"Hey, this is dumb! You can skip step B and C if you simply did this and that."* Naturally, the reaction from the establishment was, *"Behave! We have been doing this almost before your parents were born, and it's a refined process that has been proven to work over and over. Just come to work and do what you are told."* The reaction? "WE QUIT!" You see, it's abhorrent to a higher consciousness to do inefficient processes, when it "knows better." Many corporations were seeing this effect, and it was even making the pages of internal memos about how to treat the new generation. You see, the Indigo Kids were now growing up and were seeing better ways to do things.

The evolution of consciousness has already begun, and it's easy to spot. It comes in a package that looks like *rebellion over old systems, in every aspect of our society*. Is it headstrong immature rebellion (as some call it), or is it advanced, elegant thinking that simply shows impatience at dysfunction? Let me ask you, how would you feel if you were put back in school right now, to go through hours and hours of learning something that you already knew, in a sufferingly long process that was way beneath your intelligence? Do you understand how this might create a melt-down?

Watch for major changes everywhere, for it will affect every system you think is untouchable. Politics is broken (did you notice?). They are in the playground throwing rocks as usual, and it looks old and ugly. Watch for an eventual elegance of grace with those who no longer call names and play ugly games. Instead, they will run on the premise of being good negotiators, so that they can get things done among opposing sides. What a concept! Right now, politics is a war, where winner takes all until the next round. Imagine a system in which someone would run on a win-win platform?

Big Pharma is broken, and keeps people sick and dying for monetary gain. Watch for this to fall over. Banking has already taken a "hit" for integrity reasons in the USA. Who thought that integrity would ever matter in big money? It did, and the system had to be reformatted for the next round. It was simply unconscionable to sell mortgages to people who bankers knew would lose their houses and all their assets in a few years. The "anything for a sale" system of greed collapsed. But this was the old Human nature, and it had lasted for decades and decades. Why now? "The potential winning run was on third base." The potentials were starting to change us, even before we had won the game.

Lee Carroll

LEMURIA AND ATLANTIS

This book is not about Lemuria or Atlantis. However, many Old Souls are starting to awaken to feelings about these two esoteric historic places. These newly awakened feelings are starting to be part of the New Human scenario of an *Awakened Akash*, so I feel it's time to give you the information that Kryon has disclosed about all of this.

If you are a regular listener of the Kryon free-audio recorded channellings on my website, then you already know that we have been given quite a bit of additional information about each of these concepts. It has been channelled in pieces over the years, and now I'll put it together.

There are many books written about the legendary ancient city of Atlantis, even some authored by my personal friends. Each book is a separate scenario from the others, and there are many "takes" on what happened and where Atlantis might have been. So, whatever I write here will be at odds with all of them, and I'm aware of that. There is one exception, however: *The Gaia Effect* by Monika Muranyi. Monika writes about Lemuria according to the information by Kryon. Kryon presents a very different approach to Atlantis, and one that fully addresses the issue of why there are so many different versions of what might have taken place. However, I wish to start with Lemuria, for as you will see, it may be the precursor of Atlantis.

The Land of MU

There are many esoteric maps out there, which have been drawn by inspired mapmakers, about an ancient small continent that was supposed to have existed in the middle of the Pacific Ocean. Since the beginning of the practice and philosophy of metaphysics, there have been stories of this mysterious place. Kryon has channelled that, indeed, it did exist, and this "land of MU" is called Le-MU-ria.

Many of you know that I continue to look for discoveries and facts that help support what Kryon has said through my channelling, and also to support metaphysics in general. We live in a real world of 3D, and always have. I came into this work as a skeptic, and I was always bothered by stories and historical claims that had no validation at all in our reality, or that actually went against common sense. It didn't make sense to me that most spiritual history was contradictory to itself and the world we live in today. How could that be? It separates God from us totally, and that's not how Kryon says it works.

What I teach is that all these seemingly odd things, indeed, can make sense and fit into mainstream science and history, if we look for the seed truths. From angelic forms, to devas in the forest, to the Little People of Ireland, to the Adam and Eve story, Kryon has given insights as to how these things may fit into a logical paradigm of existence, because they all have *seed truths* in 3D. Look for the metaphors and the seeds, and you may find large "aha's" of truth.

The Continent That Wasn't

Legends that remain for centuries often have a very grounded historical basis. The very fact that they continue for so long tells us that there are probably realities at the ground level of history, before Humans let the stories morph through the centuries into dramatic and far-fetched tales. It's these basic truths in history that I seek, prior to their developing into unbelievable theories that tarnish so much of metaphysics.

I started by looking at the whole idea of Lemuria: Could a continent have existed in the middle of the Pacific Ocean? According to the timeline of creation given by Kryon, certain elements of the story surrounding it had to be very recent. Not only that, but the mini-continent is gone now! So to fit Kryon's scenario, it had to be there, then disappear, all in about a hundred thousand years. That's a stretch for any logical thinker, and it's laughable to any geologist. This is often what alienates many from hearing more about esoteric things.

If this continent had existed, then today's modern geology would at least see the "footprint" of it. Geology is active history. It paints a picture of what has happened, and many read it as the "Book of Gaia." So the first thing we ask is, did it exist, and if so, where is it now? Not only that, but where is the evidence of something so big, that left us in the "blink of an eye" in geological terms?

The biggest argument comes from the experts, who will point to the fact that, if a continent had been there, it had to be an "extra" one that doesn't fit into the puzzle of Pangaea. In other words, all the large land masses of the Earth are part of a system of plate tectonics that is well known, and very obvious. If you have studied the validated science of plate tectonics, you can clearly see all the *broken pieces* of the whole land mass of Earth, as they broke apart and *drifted* around the globe on their own tectonic plates through hundreds of millions of years. The issue is that there are no missing pieces! The existing continents fit together completely to form the whole. That means that the mythical Lemurian continent doesn't even fit! It would have had to be "extra land" that somehow came into being and then disappeared again.

I have heard all kinds of esoteric answers, and the ones that make me crazy are the ones that pay no attention to reality, discouraging intelligent people from inquiring further into what actually may have happened. *"Space creatures took it."* "It disappeared into a large unknown vortex." "It was in another dimension and therefore invisible" – on and on. I ask again: How can we metaphysicians ever be believed, when our answers are so thin, calling upon other unknown worlds of reality to explain something so impactful and real in our own 3D? So, these "answers" are still further nonsense that feed the idea that this story of Lemuria is total fiction.

Another Story – The Kryon Scenario

What if it were not a continent at all, but a very large, volatile landmass, pushed up from the existing sea floor around a huge volcanic mountain? If so, where did it come from, how did it happen, and where is it now? All of these are answerable, and make sense, if you follow what Kryon has channelled.

First, you might ask: What makes this Kryon channelling different from the rest of the suppositions and intuitive ideas about Lemuria and Atlantis? The answer is "nothing, really," unless it suddenly makes sense to you. We all have our *sources* who give us intuitive information. So the only thing that makes any difference is how this information is received, and if the truth of it "rings" with you. All I can do it present it.

Kryon tells us that part of the remarkable history of the Pacific Ocean is missing in today's version of history. It revolves around something geological, called a "Hot Spot." The simple definition of a Hot Spot is an area where the molten portion of the crust of the planet has been pushed up very close to the surface. It's an anomaly, and there are only about 25 to 30 of these which exist on the planet. However, where they exist often creates wild phenomena on the surface.

Two of the most well-known Hot Spots in the USA are the islands of Hawaii and Yellowstone National Park in Wyoming. Old Faithful and other geysers in Yellowstone represent unique "plumes" of the planet around a Hot Spot. Chambers in underground caverns regularly fill with water from existing groundwater sources;

the water gets super-heated to more than boiling temperature by magma close to the surface; and the super-heated water periodically explodes upward through the surface in a geyser of steam. The system repeats for centuries in a regular fashion, until, sometime in the future, tectonic Earth movement will change this activity.

The Hawaiian islands are also volatile. Since I've been alive, the main volcano, Kilauea, on the Big Island, has erupted and created more new land than in any other place on Earth. Neighborhoods have been buried, and lava continues to pour into the ocean, even today. If you look below the surface, the Hawaiian islands are deceptive. They really are not islands at all. Instead, they are the peaks of a single huge mountain under the water. In fact, measured from the bottom (under the water) to the top, Hawaii is the largest mountain on the planet. If it somehow were pushed out of the water, it would be over 29,600 feet (9,022 meters) tall! This is the altitude where commercial airlines fly, and is higher than Mount Everest.

Hawaii straddles one of the main tectonic boundaries between east and west, right in the middle of one of the largest crustal plates on Earth – the Pacific Plate. This is one of the reasons why it is a Hot Spot. Again, a Hot Spot is an area where the molten magma is close to the surface, and has the greatest potential to be active. The boundaries of the tectonic plates also involve dramatic volcanic processes that cause eruptions, earthquakes and other volcanic actions. The Pacific Plate boundary is called the "Ring of Fire" in geology.

According to Kryon, long ago the movement of the Pacific Plate created a "bubble" of hot molten energy under Hawaii. This bubble of molten magma became trapped under the crust and, instead of exploding into a massive volcano, it began to push up the entire volcanic mountain above it that we now call Hawaii. Over time, this process slowly pushed it up so that the majority of the mountain was completely out of the water. It was immense, and presented itself as a landmass of significance, centered around Hawaii – not a group of islands, but one enormous mountain, lifted up out of the bottom of the Pacific Ocean – a mini-continent.

How large was Lemuria? This was never mentioned. But how it was *used* is one of the central themes of the Kryon information. It was one of the places where our creation seeds were active. Many times, I have presented Kryon's information about the Pleiadian influence on the creation of Humans (*Homo sapiens*), and the story of our 23 chromosomes. Some other Kryon books mention it as well. I'm not going to cover this again now; however, know this: Even mainstream science continues to look for the "missing link." Some biologist are increasingly starting to feel that *Humans didn't come from anything here.* Evolutionary evidence is missing, leaving a large gap in the lineage that supposedly created *today's 23-chromosome Human.*

Turn the page with me. On the small island of Kauai in Hawaii, there is a Hindu monastery, founded many years ago by Satguru Sivaya Subramuniyaswami, a high teacher of Hinduism. The Monastery is currently open to visitors, and besides being one of the most beautifully kept grounds I have ever seen, it is a profound spiritual place. But the one thing I wish to report in this book is why it was decided to locate the Monastery in Kauai. In the early days before the Monastery was created, Satguru channelled that Hawaii is Lemuria, and that the Pleiadians were responsible for the Humans we see today. His book, "The Lemurian Scrolls," is still available today on several Internet websites. This was the entire reason he founded the Monastery there. We have taken groups to Hawaii to enjoy the grounds, and listen to the current master, Satguru Bodhinatha Veylanswami, tell us about this amazing story – the one that Kryon had given us long before I ever came to the Monastery.

Back to the Mountain

This giant mountain, a mini-continent, was called MU, or Le-MU-ria. It was almost a pure Akashic jumping-off point for much of humanity. Kryon has indicated many times that Humans never reincarnated back onto Lemuria. One life would be lived there, and after that, returning incarnations went to other parts of the Earth to spread this new Human lineage – the seeds of the knowledge of light and dark. You might say, this was similar to the Hebrew Adam and Eve story, where God gave the knowledge of light and dark and free choice, and the lineage of few, grew into the current Human lineage we know today…with 23 chromosomes.

So Lemuria was a training ground, a place where the coexistence of Pleiadian and Human had to take place for perhaps a thousand years or more. Lemurian priests often had parents from two worlds, and lived far longer than anyone else. It's an unbelievable story, if you've never heard it, yet the Hindus have it right on the island itself, and it is echoed by some of the most profound old and validated indigenous on the planet. This is another study with which I really got involved, and I have presented it before in Kryon books. If you think this is a very strange premise, I have one even stranger: The Pleiadians never left! Some are still in the teaching areas, just barely "under the surface" of our reality. Impossible? Read on.

The Ancient Ones – Still Here?

Turn the page again. There are several places on the planet where many are convinced that the Pleiadians, our divine seed biology, still exist in some form. Some of these places are very far apart, and some are sacred areas to the indigenous. However, we have held our Summer Light Conferences in one of these places, over and over: Mount Shasta in California. For decades and decades, people have gathered in this area to see the "lights on the mountain" and to feel the energy that is there. It's profound for many, and they are aware that, indeed, there could be esoteric portals of some kind. The anomalies there are not subtle, and the energy in this mountain keeps the area busy with esoteric, metaphysical tourists from all over the Earth. This is also the basis for the "Telos" books, written by Aurelia Louise Jones.

There's another place like this in the "Red Center" of Australia. Uluru (Ayers Rock) is so sacred to the Aboriginal people, that there are places you are not allowed to go, or ever fly over in a helicopter! The land belongs to them, and they manage it in association with the Australian national park service. The Aboriginal Elders, for the most part, are in charge of who goes where, around this sacred rock. The reason you can't go to some places? *The Ancient Ones with names you can't pronounce* are still there. To these people, the "Ancient Ones" are the Pleiadians. This is their creation story, as we have found it also to be on Easter Island (Rapa Nui) – more later on this.

Back to Lemuria

So, there is this giant mountain sticking up in the middle of the Pacific Ocean. It's not a continent by definition, but it's large. This could be the seed truth of the legends of old, and would explain how such a thing might exist. But it doesn't exist now. What happened? Kryon tells us that, as the bubble vented over time, it slowly lowered the mountain. It begin to sink. Hawaii's main volcanic system is defined as consisting of *Shield Volcanos*. This isn't the typical volcano that erupts in a giant explosion, such as Krakatoa. Instead, it may have a main caldera, but also pockets of eruptions pop out of the side and flow into the sea. This keeps it from building up to a one-time major explosion, such as we witnessed with Mount Saint Helens in the state of Washington (on the eastern side of the "Ring of Fire" boundary of the Pacific Plate). Whatever method vented the Lemurian bubble is not known, but the mountain started to retreat to its original position, sitting flat on the bottom of the ocean. Slowly, it began to "sink" and the inhabitants were in a panic.

Before we tell the rest of the channelled story, I will now tell you about some of my revelation and research. I have told this before in my writing, but now it fits into an incredible possibility of Lemuria being real, so again I relate it to you.

I talked to a few geologists about the entire potential of Hawaii being pushed up by the Hot Spot. The answers I got were very similar: *"NO. No way. There is simply no evidence of it."* Then I asked, "What evidence would there be, if it had happened?" The answer was: *"If there had been something like this, all the evidence would now be completely under water and long ago washed away or eroded to nothing."* So, there is no evidence of it in known geology, but the possibility of it is not out of the question, although doubtful (according to everyone I talked to). So I'm stuck with a "far out" truth from my channelling, and I felt that I would have to live with that, since there was nothing anyone could offer to help validate it.

The Hotel Room Experience

I'm tired, and relaxing after a channelling in a city somewhere in the States. The date and time escapes me, since so often these things blur together over time. I'm in my hotel room, and I do what so many others do – I start surfing the channels of my hotel TV. Clicking past the silly or violent shows, I finally settle on a documentary in progress on the Discovery Channel, called How The Earth Was Made. I'm drifting in my consciousness into a sleep state, until I clearly hear the words *"Hot Spot"* coming from the TV speaker. I'm wide awake! My attention is riveted: The documentary is explaining recent geological discoveries within Yellowstone Park, a geological Hot Spot (remember?). They are saying that mysterious giant linear scratches in many of the rocks have now been identified and explained. They were caused by glaciers which formed long ago when Yellowstone was lifted high up into the atmosphere by a "bubble in the mantle of the Earth around the Hot Spot!" An animation they created shows how Yellowstone was pushed up. They go on to show the hidden calderas all over Yellowstone where the imprints of giant volcanoes had been.

Did I just hear what I thought I heard? Yellowstone was pushed up so high that glaciers formed! Then it subsided to being almost entirely flat again, as we know it today. That's the exact scenario described by Kryon about Lemuria around Hawaii. This was astonishing news to me, and I was also perplexed that some of the educators I spoke to didn't know about it. I knew this wasn't proof of Lemuria. But it's great validation of the possibility that what happened in one Hot Spot, also could have happened in another, for the same geological reasons. To me, this made it real in today's geological science.

Finally, I got a fun "wink" from Spirit. I got to studying Google Maps. Most of the ocean around Hawaii has been mapped years ago for depth and geological attributes. We know the flat areas, submerged mountains, and even another Hawaiian island being formed now that will someday emerge ... all this around the Hot Spot. So the mapping of the ocean is available on Google, and you can see it clearly when you go to the Hawaiian Islands map. However, to really see what I saw, back out the view on your screen to include a very large area around Hawaii. When I did this, I stared at it and looked closer. Are those *stretch marks* around the island? YIKES! They are! What if the striations of depth and shape that Google is clearly showing on the ocean floor, are stretch marks from the mountain having raised up very long ago in history, and then sunk back down in the last 100,000 years? Who knows? But it's there to see!

Atlantis – The Beginning

The question that arrives first about Atlantis is this: Could the slow sinking of Lemuria, actually be Atlantis? Everything fits, since Kryon's history of Lemuria clearly shows it subsiding, and Kryon describes the panic of the civilization there. It was slow, however, and not like some of the Akashic remembrances that many have of explosions, horror, and death. But it's still something dramatic that could be recorded in our beginning Akashic records.

Kryon's answer to this question, "*Is Lemuria, Atlantis?*" is on record in several places: "*Not exactly.*" When we asked Kryon in a Q&A session, "*Where is Atlantis?*", Kryon's response was, "*Which one?*" Oops! There was more than one? Kryon says there were many, and three main ones that the Akash of humanity remembers more than the others. (*Hear the Lemurian Sisterhood channelling June 8, 2015*[1]).

Kryon continues to elaborate, calling this whole Atlantis experience, *The Sinking Island Syndrome*. Kryon goes on to tell an elaborate and powerful story about Lemurians, as they evacuated their own sinking island of MU. When Lemuria started to sink, many left, since there was no reason to believe it would stop sinking. To the residents, it was going under. Today we realize that it did not sink completely, for the islands of Hawaii are the tops of the sunken mountain. Back then, there was panic and most of the residents of this mini-continent left over the years. It was a slow movement, but it was frightening to lose land every single day to the sea.

Off to Other Islands

To me, it's really interesting to examine this evacuation, according to Kryon, for in it there is more validation to be seen. There was really no place for the Lemurian civilization to go! There was no other land around them, and so they took to the canoes, or other boats they built, and followed the currents, hopefully to other land. Indeed, many found other islands, and the stories we get from the Elders, of where they were supposed to have landed, are startling in their profundity as they validate what Kryon has told us.

1   www.kryon.com/34-1

The winds and the currents took most of them south, according to Kryon – far to the south. Kryon says that many ended up at Easter Island (Rapa Nui), and others ended up in New Zealand. Both of these locations have been part of my personal research in recent years, and I have interviewed some of the indigenous at both places regarding their beliefs about their ancient origins. The most profound is on Rapa Nui. For there, we have almost the exact story that Kryon tells.

The Rapa Nui have a wonderful story of the seven voyagers: They tell of a far away King who had a sinking island. The King sent seven voyagers to find another island home, based on one of his Shaman's visions of a far away island to the south. The seven men followed the Shaman's vision and they found Rapa Nui! They returned to the King, reported the news, and the evacuation began. This is the Rapa Nui story of how they got there. Rapa Nui is almost straight down from Hawaii in the Pacific Ocean, in the southern hemisphere. Today, there are seven of those famous Easter Island statues (called Moai) on Rapa Nui, facing toward Hawaii. The rest of the Moai (over 800 of them) face inward toward the center of the island, representing their ancestors watching over them.

To make this even more fun for me, the Rapa Nui firmly claim the Pleiadians as their star Ancestors, and it's the first thing they showed us when we met with them. They have a small ceremonial statue that represents the Pleiadian connection! So their story is identical to the Kryon channelling about a sinking Lemuria, except for the timing of it. But wait, there is a puzzle here, and the solution to this puzzle was given by Kryon during a channelling on Rapa Nui itself.

The puzzle? These seven voyagers who left their sinking home, navigated the best they could, using an ancient but accurate system: The stars. They had been doing this for centuries and knew the constellations well. But as they went South, they had a brand new collection of stars in the sky, and slowly lost the ones they knew. The North Star vanished completely (gasp), and the Big Dipper was gone, too. The main configuration in the sky became the Southern Cross and the associated constellations around it. It was critical to take bearings, so they wouldn't go in circles, yet they had never seen the stars in the southern hemisphere. There is only so much you can do to navigate with the sun and moon in the middle of the ocean. How did they do this?

To make this story even more remarkable, they had to navigate back to Hawaii again, to give the news to the king! How was this done without knowledge of the southern hemisphere's sky? In Kryon's Rapa Nui channelling, it was explained that their Pleiadian teachers had given them full knowledge of what the sky looked like in the southern hemisphere. Again, this is not proof of anything, but it answers valid 3D questions about the very real history of Rapa Nui's lineage – as told by the Rapa Nui indigenous.

The second place that Lemurians found (which Kryon spoke about), was New Zealand. It's harder to validate this, since the current Māori indigenous of New Zealand are the second or third civilization from the original settlers (according to Kryon's channelling, and also some Māori Elders). However, circumstantial evidence abounds. First, they celebrate the appearance of the Seven Sisters (Pleiades) constellation in the sky, in the same way as the Hawaiians do (their New Year). What a coincidence! And – the name of their celebration is Matariki, only a few letters different from the Hawaiian celebration, Makahiki! The Seven Sisters cluster is one of the few constellations that appears in both the northern and southern hemisphere sky.

New Zealand is also a very close neighbor of Australia, yet there are no Aboriginal settlements at all. Instead, they are Polynesian.

This is odd, since the Aboriginals have been in Australia for at least 30,000 years (validated by the Australian government). You would think that during that time, the Aboriginals would have found New Zealand and settled there, too. I believe that the Aboriginals found New Zealand early on, but they know and respect the energy of the land and what cultural boundaries mean. They call it *Aboriginal Law* and it's part of their culture, even today. So they probably left and never settled, leaving it to the Lemurians they found there.

Finally, the Māori claim that they are Polynesian and come from "the Pacific Ocean." However, the word for *Pacific Ocean* in the Māori language is (ready?) – Hawaii!

The Sinking Island Syndrome

Over the many years of evacuating the main sinking island of Lemuria, Kryon says that Lemurian culture settled many other islands around the planet. It was natural, and it was in their Akash – the desire to live comfortably on an island. Also, most of the islands that were selected in the oceans of the planet were volcanic. This is how they lived in Lemuria, and it was natural to them, and felt very comfortable.

Over the years, many of these other islands either exploded, sank, or displayed other types of destructive endings. So, over generations and generations, many former Lemurians were being given remembrances of multiple sinking island experiences. This laid the foundation of the potential that so many Light Workers and Old Souls claim – to be from Atlantis. *The Sinking Island Syndrome*, therefore, may be etched in the Akashic memories of many esoterically-minded people, especially the ones who read this book.

Kryon tells us that there really may only have been three actual cultures named "Atlantis." It also makes sense that, if one was destroyed, there might be others of the same name. We even do this in our culture today, naming new things after old ones in history. Survivors might settle another island and create "The New Atlantis" to honor the ones they lost. What if they then lost the second one, too? Can you see the buildup in the Akashic memory record of "trauma related to sinking islands"? First Lemuria, then another and another and another.

So, Kryon tells us that Akashic remembrances of a sinking island go back to the original Lemurian experience, and that all through Human history, there have been other sinking islands that caused dramatic memories. Some of them sank quickly, and others did not. Kryon also gives a hint that the ones actually called "Atlantis" were quite young, as history goes. One of them was not volcanic at all, but was quickly covered by water in the Mediterranean Sea during an earthquake (according to the channelling).

Hopefully, if you have not heard all of this before, you can start thinking about the seeds of truth that it contains. Combined with scientific precedent, indigenous historical validation, and the common sense of it all, the land of MU may have actually existed, as did Atlantis ... many times over.

Lee Carroll

Chapter One

The New Human Part 1

When Kryon first started talking about The New Human, I thought I knew what the messages would be like. However, I was not prepared for all the information that follows in this book. It seems that it could be a complete re-write of the Human Being, or more accurately, Human Nature. These first two chapters set the stage for the rest of the book.

Kryon gives seven attributes of the New Human and I believe, the most profound of the attributes are the ones that deal with relationships – with God, with yourself, and even with the Earth, itself. I'm beginning to realize that I will have to rethink what Human spiritual evolution actually means.

Lee Carroll

Chapter One

"The New Human Part 1"

Kryon Live Channelling
Given in Valencia, Spain

September 19, 2015

Greetings, dear ones, I am Kryon of Magnetic Service. Some will say, this message is a summary, but I've chosen to deliver it so that the elements are together in a way that they have not been before. Between this night and the next, I will present a series called "The New Human." It's a beautiful message, and it's benevolent. The message is about you.

Dear ones, you would not be sitting here today unless you cared about this subject. You wouldn't be sitting here, trying to understand something that is often elusive information, about what's happening on the planet, unless you cared. My partner says that you are in a shift. It's actually more than that. You are approaching an energy that you've never been in before. This is not a cycle. Everything on the planet to this point has been a cycle, just like your weather, and just like astronomy, which is in a predictable system. The Earth goes through cycles, but this is not one of them.

Everything changes gradually. You look outside and you hear about the changes of weather over time. You look at the news and you realize there is something different going on from what has happened in the past. My message from the beginning was to get ready for this change, and the biggest change will be within humanity.

The New Human

Human nature is about to shift, and it will be the first time in any of your history where this has happened. More than a shift in Human nature, it is about to become new. Psychologists will tell you that Human nature is static – that is to say, that it does not change. It simply "comes with being a Human Being." Part of the study of psychology itself, requires that it is static so that it can be studied, and then many can benefit from the gathered knowledge. History reinforces this, and it will show that Human nature is responsible for the same kinds of fear and survival instinct over and over, and that it never changes. History repeats itself in all its dysfunction, drama and war, and you can count on Human nature being the same. Often, when the very phrase "Human nature" is used, it's in a negative connotation. This very fact shows you that even scholars realize that the intrinsic nature of Humans is flawed.

The idea of a real change in Human nature is, therefore, not seen as possible by the experts. It never changed, so why would it now? So this coming change is a tough idea to accept, for those who are scientifically minded, for there is no evidence yet of what we are calling "The Big Shift." There is only evidence so far of *coincidental* shift, because these things happen slowly. Sometimes shift goes so slowly that you are not even aware of it, but it's starting now.

The New Attributes

I would like to itemize the kinds of attributes to expect as the *New* Human starts to appear. You are entering into a new energy that has never been here before, and these attributes of what is happening will eventually change Human nature itself. It's going to change everything about you, and civilization on the planet. Some will like it, and some will not. Change always does that. It is never easy. We're going to start with four of seven attributes. I will give you the balance of them tomorrow.

I've spoken about some of these concepts before, but never in a list like this. I want you to see how profound this is. Dear Old Soul, are you ready to participate in the evolution of humanity? This will be an evolution taking you to a place that has not existed before – a wisdom the Earth has never seen, and the slow building of a new kind of harmonious peace on the planet. This peace on Earth will simply come along with higher evolved thinking, and is just the beginning of a constant, growing and evolving Human nature. The very consciousness of humanity is about to slowly shift. It's starting to show itself in small ways, but you're sitting here because some of you feel it, don't you? Something is different.

ONE

The first attribute is The Human's Relationship with God. It's the basic one. Whatever you wish to call *God*, the concept is *The Creative Source of all things*. Some have called this concept *God*, and some have said *Spirit*. Others say, *Source*.

Most of humanity believes that their consciousness does not stop at death. Every belief system, even fairly obscure ones, believe and teach that the soul continues somehow after corporeal death. Therefore, you could safely say that most of humanity believes in an after-life of some kind. In general, eighty to ninety percent of humanity does not believe they stop consciousness when they die. This is a strong acknowledgement of an *intuitive God inside*. Even still, many intellectual thinkers believe it is simply the Human survival instinct extended, and that it is *wishful thinking*. But throughout the ages, it has instead become the basis for faith, healing, love, peace, compassion, and major spiritual thinking of billions of Humans. So, no matter what the spiritual belief, the idea of existing beyond corporeal life has had strong evidence through miracles and intuition. It was also the intuitive idea of the first spiritual systems recorded on the planet. Life does not end when you die!

So, who or what is God? How can a Human deal with the idea of a greater power "in the sky"? What has happened in the past regarding this subject, is part of an old Human nature. Humans have created a God or Gods that emulate Humans. Humans only have one model of consciousness, and it is themselves. So God, then, becomes a supreme power that has Human attributes. This has created a current system, over thousands of years, where God has become like a dysfunctional parent.

God loves you beyond measure, you are told, yet *He* will send you to burn in a dark place forever, if you do something improper. Add to that, there is no consensus of what is "proper." So you have a God who is much, much less benevolent than you are with your own children! Does this sound like the beautiful, benevolent God that I speak of, or does it sound like something man-made? Indeed, for most of the planet, the very essence of God is the essence of Human nature!

What history has given you is this concept: Human nature is also God nature. Therefore, even in your modern belief systems to this day, there were wars in heaven and fallen angels. God has anger and punishment and judgment, just like Human nature. Whoever you are, reading this or hearing this, think: Does this really make any spiritual sense? Killing each other, and creating wars through disagreement and competition is what Humans do. It is not what God does.

I don't want to offend anyone here, or hearing this later, but the benevolence of the Creative Source, the One who created the Universe, does not "think" like a Human! The nature of God is pure. It fills every molecule of the atmosphere of this planet with love. It is as pure as anything you can ever imagine. It is beyond anything that you can conceive of, in its benevolence and its care for you. Spirit sees you as family, temporarily on the planet, and eventually coming back. God does not feature punishment – ever! This is a Human concept! God does not have Human attributes of anger or disappointment. God does not have low consciousness, or argue with itself. God is not dysfunctional. You are! That's old Human nature, and it's about to change and become more God-like.

The relationship to Spirit (God) is going to change. Some of you are going to start feeling this, and will be wide-open to this change. You're going to finally understand and realize that the God of the Universe is inside you, and the hand of God is before you, waiting for you to take it.

This is a metaphor that means that a personal God is ready to affirm a relationship with you that will create day-by-day compassion and joy, and an evolvement in Human nature within you. You will begin to act differently because you will change in many ways. When you vibrate higher with an evolved DNA, you will have greater awareness. That's basic.

The benevolence and greater wisdom of God will start to be obvious to you, and therefore, will be with you in your life. The way you act will be different. You will study the Masters and see what an advanced Human nature they had, and you will realize they had a totally different consciousness. You will begin to emulate that and many around you will see it. The New Human will know who God is, and relate to it, and not be apart from it. That's one.

TWO

The second is Awareness of Self. Who are you? What is your purpose? Right now, I'll tell you that your lives have all been about *survival*. Oh, you may believe in these kinds of esoteric things that you are here for today, but as you live with others on the planet, you just survive. Whether you're in school or going to work, or just living on Earth, you are only surviving. Old Soul, you're careful who you tell about these things, aren't you? That's so you can survive without drama or bias or trouble. Did you realize how much you are in survival? Even in a very sophisticated society, you are in basic survival – just like thousands of years ago.

Dear ones, how do you feel about yourself? We have spoken of this before, many times. As you have a closer walk with Spirit, the thing you call *SELF* will change. You will be less afraid. You will become more calm and peaceful about everything. You will not be evangelistic with what you believe. Instead, you will *practice* what you believe and be a much kinder person. Anger will start to pass away, and the things that irritate you will become far less. You will be more balanced than ever before, and others will want to be with you because of it. You will slowly become the New Human.

Instead of being ready to argue with everyone over something you strongly believe in, you will, instead, know how to be silent and listen. There will be compassion, instead of judgment. It's almost a full reversal of what Human nature has created so far. You will be balanced!

Finally, when it comes to *SELF*, you'll start to evaluate yourself, and you'll say, *"I have a right to be here in this new energy. I was born for this, and now here I am!"* How many of you are getting this – really understanding this? Know this: You deserve to be here, and it's not an accident or randomness of nature that you exist. God loves you and knows every hair on your head. There's a benevolent bridge between you and Spirit, and you can breathe a sigh of relief about everything in your life.

Listen: As you review your life, you haven't done anything *wrong*. Nothing! You have made choices, and God honors the free choices you have made. That's the design! This is how Humans evolve and learn. There will be no punishment for what you think you might have done. You are able to forgive yourself for what you've done, because God does not see things as you do. From God, there is no forgiveness needed. You are magnificent in the eyes of the Creator! This is far different from the spiritual systems on this planet who offer you the "rules of God," and the judgment and punishment of a dysfunctional Deity, who would torture his children forever, if they break man-made rules. Connect the dots and use some spiritual logic! God is not an extension of Human nature.

Dear ones, you are here working with the energy of the planet, and what you do tests the energy and changes it. You're not here as a test of your soul. You didn't come to Earth to suffer! Your soul is forever and belongs to God and always will – always will! Love is the source – the only source, and everything is based around it. You are going to have to re-write who God is in your life, and finally see that there is a hand out to you – a metaphor that invites you to see *God inside* you. Is it you? Do you feel it? Do you feel the shift and the change away from anger, hatred, and frustration?

Old Soul, you represent the Human who is finally coming out of the cave of survival, looking around, and realizing that there are more elegant things than just surviving from day to day. Love builds a vital and energetic bridge from Human to Human, and compassion is the result. Compassionate action [action by Humans based in compassion and caring] is what will change basic Human nature forever.

Who are you? You are part of the elegant system of creation.

THREE

Changes within the Compassion of Humanity: How do you feel about others on your planet? Are you alone in your "bubble" and just surviving, or are you part of the whole of humanity? What is your responsibility? What's happening on your news? For the first time in Human history, there is going to be a puzzle about the refugees pouring into your areas [remember, this is being channelled in Spain in 2015]. All of the nations around you have this issue, some more and some less. There is horror and unbalance in certain societies on your planet, and families are racing out of their countries into yours. They are afraid for their lives, and the lives of their families, and they push toward you in great numbers. This was foretold to you, when we spoke of the darkness coming forward in these days of shift, causing great changes. This is the direct result of having more light being developed on the planet. Dark consciousness is acting out, and trying its best to pull the planet backwards, back into survival.

What can you do? How is your society going to afford it? Where are you going to put these people, if you let them in? Are they welcome, or are they not welcome? Will you let them die on the border? This is a Human nature problem and the solutions will be different from any solutions that have ever been. In the past, you have simply ignored this kind of thing, and have let your government handle it. But suddenly, there are photos of dead children on your news, and families perishing, trying to escape.

Right now, there are no viable solutions, since you have never developed a compassionate plan for this. It's so new, that there is no infrastructure for any of it, and no funding. There is much frustration and fear, and there are some Humans who are practicing the old Human nature, saying, *"It's their problem, not ours. Let them solve their own issues."*

Part of the New Human will feature a totally different reaction from that of the past: Compassionate action will start to be seen on a mass level, and there will be those who will work on solutions, because they see the refugees as *Human family*. A more benevolent and soft consciousness will say, *"Look into the eyes of the children. They're just like ours."* Compassion will then start to create wise solutions that are fair, and this will lessen the suffering.

In any shift, there is objection to new thinking, and fear will be the result. There are many who will say, *"I understand, but if we let them in, they are infiltrating terrorists within their numbers."* Dear ones, this is not a reason to turn them away, but instead, this is a reason to find a solution to sort out the terrorists. It is well within your abilities to do this, but you need to fund it. You will figure this out.

Solutions that make sense will slowly be developed by those who are starting to think differently and who are using compassion as their goal and their guidelines for legislation and action. This is new! As Humans consider how to implement compassionate thinking, solutions that have never been needed before, or tried, will manifest themselves. This is basic metaphysics, where the action of conscious focus, then creates the answer. It almost is like the answers are "released" instead of developed – like they were there all along, but higher consciousness was the key that turned the lock of wisdom and awareness.

There will be intellectuals and linear thinkers who will say, *"Well, compassionate action hasn't worked before, and it's not going to get us the money we need to afford to fund this issue!"* They will call you esoteric fools, and roll their eyes at anyone who thinks you can "love everyone into solution." Welcome to old Human nature. They don't know what they don't know. Just because they have never seen something, doesn't mean it doesn't exist. Wisdom and invention are like this. It lies there hiding, ready to be discovered by those who are courageous enough to shift their thinking.

Is it possible to create funding for situations that are outside the scope of anything you have seen before? Why should this be any different from your technical advancements? You actually "schedule" your future for inventions that haven't happened yet! Yet, you feel that it's impossible to create answers to social issues. That's because social issues are ones that push the envelope of an evolving Human nature.

Can it be done? Can countries start something that has never been done before, which will help those who are not part of their own societies? How about a "department of compassion" in each government, which is funded the same way weapons are? The answer is yes, you can do this, but majority consensus is the key, and that's what is starting to change world-wide among first world cultures. If you want it bad enough, it can be done.

Every objection to this issue can be met and solved with the New Human, who looks first at the compassionate action attributes of the puzzle and thinks *out of the box* on how to solve it. Many of the solutions may surprise you, and each country has its own ways of doing it, but all countries are now part of it. It's the first time in history that multiple countries are all involved in the same issue of pure compassion.

I wish you could see what it's going to be like in fifty years. You'll look backwards, and refer to it as the great compassion experiment, or the great integration. Then you'll realize that this massive historical attempt saved many, many lives without the negative warnings that were given. Those saved will be able to give back in ways you haven't even considered yet. The mold will be cast for the future, and countries will be proud of their ability to work a humanitarian puzzle in a very personal and positive way. It goes way beyond "foreign aid," or even the work of your United Nations. For it will be an intrinsic part of each government.

There may be some things coming that may surprise you, for light will win over darkness and Human nature will not rise up in negative uncaring ways like it used to. You will no longer fear others the way you do now, and you will begin to rise out of survival. Dear ones, I want you to breathe. Is there anything too complex for God? What does your heart say? You are the New Human.

FOUR

Here is the final attribute for this day: Integration of the Shift.

What does the New Human feel within the new energy? It's almost everything I've given you today and more. The issues are in front of you regarding a major shift, yet so many just see these things as more problems on the planet. *"Here comes another problem,"* they say. The weather is shifting – *"Here comes another problem."* Most of humanity does not understand that the shift is actually creating these things.

The New Human will start to evolve. The ones who sit here as Old Souls, and who are reading this, are the ones who will have the answers first – not just those in Spain, but the family of Spirit throughout all the countries on the planet.

What do you think of the new energy? Let's be honest, Human Being. You signed up for this current life of yours. You made an appointment for this. You're in the right place at the right time, and the shift is here as designed. Energetically, it's frustrating. You're seeing things you didn't see before, and it's frightening. You're seeing pure evil sweep over certain cultures, and you don't understand it. You didn't expect it. Did you know that this is the first time in Human history in which you're about to fight a battle with evil? It's not a battle with another country or culture. Instead, it's a very low consciousness group that has no borders and no common language. It represents very old ways of thinking, and it depends on fear to exist. It wants to frighten you into staying the same as you were before, and we predicted this scenario in 2012.

We told you that when the shift came, light would increase on the planet. That's a metaphor for enlightenment and new thinking. Old souls would start to feel it and be frustrated, because things were not the same. Change often leads to fear and misunderstanding. We told you that the darkness of old thinking and ancient ways would take advantage of this, and would pull together everything they could, to stop the shift of light. Those were our words back then, and these are now the things on your news today.

You think this is all a surprise, a coincidence, perhaps? It's right on schedule, Old Soul! You see, light is going to win and the New Human is going to have new wisdom to provide that light. It's not just more war this time. It may, instead, be the final battle.

It's frustrating when you have changes. Some of you are feeling health issues, because your actual body is shifting and moving toward a new vibration. Some of you are not sleeping well. Some of you are worried and don't even know why! That's what happens when Human nature starts to shift. The huge differences that are happening make the New Human uncomfortable.

So, how does it feel, so far? I'm telling the truth today, and many are nodding their heads in agreement. What can you do about this discomfort? I want you to relax a bit right now: Be still, and know that you are a piece of God. I wish you to know that everything you see around you is part of a massive correction of the balance between dark and light. Over time, you'll see it, and you'll feel it. Some of you in this room may even have a healing, in these two days. It will be a healing from anger, hatred, and frustration. You will realize you can throw that all away, and begin to understand that God cares about you, the New Human. You are here as an Old Soul on this planet for a reason – for a reason!

And so it is.

"Synchronicity is always on the move, and is dynamic, depending on how often you listen to intuitive potentials that are given to you. There will always be people for you to meet. There are always good things available. Synchronicity is a benevolent energy that is designed to help you. Are you taking advantage of this?"

Kryon

Chapter Two

The New Human Part 2

As I indicated, it gets harder now. The last of the list of attributes is multi-dimensional and interactive. That means that when one is changed, it changes each of the other ones.

In addition, there really is no beginning or end (as in a normal list). As Kryon says, "It's hard to put a circle in a list!" So get ready for a little bit of time travel, where Kryon will leap around a bit as he describes why we should expect benevolent change!

Lee Carroll

Chapter Two

"The New Human Part 2"

Kryon Live Channelling
Given in Valencia, Spain

September 20, 2015

Greetings, dear ones, I am Kryon of Magnetic Service. Before we begin with any teaching, I want to sit for a moment with you. I want to re-energize the entourage from Spirit, who is here. It's still here from the day before. Some of you could feel it when you came into the room today, and you knew it was still here. These esoteric things are energetic. They require discernment and sensitivity to discern, just like the message that's going to follow.

The entourage who comes with me is benevolent. It does not sit here expecting things from you. It's a group that is always defined by energy of what is here. It's all melded together, and it knows you, and it knows itself. The entourage is specific to this room and it sits and watches and participates with you. It's here for support. If you should have a thought, an intuition, or an awakening, or a healing, it's ready to help you with all of it. So this is a very good time and place for decisions about your relationship with yourself, with God, and with others.

Last night we began a channelling, and tonight we finish. The subject is the seven attributes of the New Human. Now, there are a lot more than seven attributes, so the seven we examine are only for those who sit here and need to hear it. This is the way of channelling, for it responds to the energy of the now.

Hundreds of Lightworkers sit in front of me [speaking of the Spain meeting]. This is the energy we address, from the moment my partner sat here yesterday, and as we continue today. This channelling is specific to the energy of those who sit in front of me, and who are listening and reading. I'm speaking to you! I expected you. I know what you bring to this discussion, since I know your energies. I see the joy and the celebration among you. I see some of the frustrations, and the unbalance because of them. Spirit sees it all, and in benevolent ways, we desire to take your hand and help you with all of it. We know your name!

Yesterday, we gave you four attributes of the New Human. They were easily understandable, for they were linear. Yesterday, I could list the four and categorize them for you, but tonight, I cannot. In linear counting, I gave you four of the seven, and you would think there would be three remaining. However, this is not correct, since the three that are remaining are actually in a circle. It's an interactive circle, and the three together represent a conundrum – a puzzle that has the riddle of interactive relativity. In other words, one thing affects another. So, therefore, you cannot list them in a linear fashion, because they all change together, and that spoils the linear idea of a list, since the names keep changing.

It's hard to put a circle in a list! To a multidimensional mind, it's not an issue, but you wish to see things in a linear way. So I can list the three for you, but I want you to imagine a circle as we go, and all three parts are at the center. If you affect one, you affect the other two. In fact, there won't really be a list, and the names of the three swap and change constantly.

Indeed, there will appear to be three subjects here, but it's not that way. Even as I name them to you, which I must do, you will set up a linearity of what to expect, based on the names I give you. You will wish to put them in boxes that are separate, but you can't. These things are not what you think. Here are the three remaining in the circle that creates this conundrum for you: Relationships, Earth Energy, and Ancestor Energy. They are together. If you talk about one, you talk about all. The New Human needs to see this. Let us begin.

FIVE – SIX – SEVEN

What is your relationship to your own Akash? Do you have a relationship at all? The New Human will. The New Human will have a remembrance of energy of the past. This is a remembrance that you will count on for help, instead of it being a blockage or difficult karmic energy. It's a relationship that is personal to only you. I have told you that you are your own ancestor. Think about it: If you have reincarnated in the same place, over and over, the chances are very great that you have been part of your own family tree. You are, therefore, your own ancestor. So, if I ask you, what is your relationship to your ancestors, I'm really asking you about how you feel about your own soul participating in your own past.

How long have you been reincarnating in this area [speaking of Spain]? What if you are several of your own ancestors? What is your relationship today with the Akash that contains all three? What if there were more than three? What if they [your past lives] were different genders?

Now, there are intellectuals here who will try to take this apart and in their linearity, they will confuse biology with the Akash. We are not talking about direct biological ancestry as much as Akashic family. Your Akash is separate from your biological ancestry, but occasionally, they overlap. Occasionally, you might even be your own great-grandfather. Are you confused yet? What is your relationship with this?

For instance, you might carry the biological imprint of your great-grandmother, or great-grandfather, and actually carry their attributes, talents and looks. Yet, your immediate past life might be from another culture! I do this to show you that this entire discussion is complex and can't be linear. So you might say, you have a soul lineage that is sometimes different than your chemical lineage, but they exist together in your body.

Let's extend this. What is your relationship with the stars? Is there one? Have you isolated yourself to believe that you are simply from the Earth? Do you believe that you evolved from the dirt of the Earth? You'd be surprised, dear ones, for you carry multidimensional DNA, and it is literally the essence of the stars! Is it possible you have family that is not on the planet? We speak of seed-parents. How do you feel about that? Is it too strange?

Let me tell you something. The New Human will be relaxed with this idea, and will join with many of the ancients who believe that the Seven Sisters' Pleiadian energy is that which seeded the Earth. It did so with spiritual benevolence and cosmic purpose. Let's go one step further. If that premise is true, did the Pleiadians themselves have seeds from other star systems? If so, are you related to the seeds of your seed parents? Is your Human Akash limited to Earth lifetimes? If you have the beginning imprint from the stars, is it also part of your Human Akash? If it is, what about the seeds of their seeds? Who started them?

How long has this been going on? We've told you this before: Planet Earth is young – very young. You are the new ones in the galaxy and the seeds you have from the stars are ancient. Other life is far, far older than humanity, and had civilizations like yours before life on Earth even started!

So think about this: Who are you? What's in your Akash? What if you are timeless? Perhaps you're not just an old *Earth* soul. What if you are a *Universal* soul? What would that mean to you today, if it were true? Well, Old Soul, it's true! Inside you is a growing awareness that you're from the stars, and are very close to the Creative Source of the Universe itself. The New Human will be comfortable with that.

It gets more complicated. What is your relationship to planet Earth? Now, we don't mean that which is the dirt of the Earth. Your planet has an energy of benevolence that works with the consciousness of humanity. It's called Gaia. Beautiful Gaia! Some of you know this profoundly. You'll go into the countryside and feel it and it speaks to you. You may sit down by a tree or perhaps a stream – and the wind in the trees whispers to you. *"We know you – All is well."* Gaia knows you as we do. What is your relationship? Do you even have one? Does it overlap with your Akash?

The New Human will know of the relationship to the Earth. We have told you before about Gaia's influence on your consciousness. I am Kryon, the Magnetic Master. This is the name I give you, because we have taught you that the magnetic grid of your planet is necessary for your very life. It actually postures your consciousness [allows for it to exist]. We began to channel to you almost three decades ago, and the first information we gave you was, that the magnetic grid would shift and change, allowing new Human consciousness to develop. This was in order to allow a new Human nature to evolve, and even a new DNA efficiency to begin to develop. By the way, it did – the grid shifted exactly as we said, and this is now science.

Your physical DNA chemistry may look the same for centuries, but the multidimensional portion will be changing. The magnetic grid is intrinsically related to your consciousness, and it is Gaia energy. Do you ever talk to Gaia? Do you realize that that's ALL the Ancients did? There was tremendous respect for Earth-energy with almost every ancient civilization, and it was even the seed energy that the Greeks used to create their mythological Gods. Gaia was the grandmother of Zeus, the highest of their Gods. Gaia was the highest energy before anything else in most of the ancient civilizations, for Gaia has a consciousness of its own that can be felt, and it's one that supports you. So, again, do you think it's totally separate from the other esoteric relationships you have, or could it be melded somehow?

Now let me put this forward: What is your relation to the Ancients? Not the immediate ones that we spoke of earlier, but the ones that were here thousands of years ago? Did you know they knew about Gaia? Did you know they celebrated magnetics? You probably didn't put that together, did you? The Ancients of this planet, in their ceremonies, would often give honor to the east, the south, the north, and the west [not in that order]. What were they doing? They were celebrating the directions of the magnetics of the planet. They were sensing the energy of the grids, which helped to give them balance and life.

Did you know that many of the Ancients actually hunted the animals they needed for food, using grid lines? This was possible, because they knew the animals tended to create paths that aligned with the directions of the compass [migration lines]. The Ancients counted on Gaia for survival in ways that you've lost in your day. I ask it again, what is your relationship to the Ancestors, and to Gaia? Do you see the puzzle before you? This is not three attributes we are discussing, but rather a circle of blended energies, and it's beautiful. I'm asking you: Who are you, really?

Relationships are interesting, and now it really gets personal: What's your relationship to the Creative Source [God]? Do you believe it's real? Do you believe that there is a single, beautiful, benevolent God who is never judging you, but who loves you? Do you have that relationship-awareness yet? What is your relationship to the smart body [Innate]? Have you ever talked to your Innate? Have you ever spoken things, knowing that the Innate within you is listening? Did you know that your Innate knows about your ancestry? Your Innate knows about your relationship to the stars, too! It gets complicated, doesn't it? Well, dear ones, it doesn't have to be.

All the things we are giving you are automatically activated, without intellectual examination, and without having to figure them out. This circle I have just described is all part of the energy of your Merkabah. All of the relationships we have mentioned: your past lives, your ancestral lineage, your Earth-energy knowledge, and your seed biology, are contained in something that is a part of you.

Dear ones, you walk around with an enormous field that is multidimensional. It is eight meters wide and is called *The Human Merkabah*. It is a beautiful esoteric blueprint of YOU. If you could see it as I do, you would see the sacred geometry within it. This is who you are, and you never have to worry about the details of any esoteric system, or figure them out. Once you commit to your belief that this is the way things work, you actually activate your own awareness.

Synchronicity is always on the move, and is dynamic, depending on how often you listen to intuitive potentials that are given to you. There will always be people for you to meet. There are always good things available. Synchronicity is a benevolent energy that is designed to help you. Are you taking advantage of this?

If you start connecting in the ways we have given you tonight, elegant, mysterious things start to come into focus. All of these things we bring you come together in a package called the New Human. It's not anything that you have to list, or write down, and the only reason we have done so tonight is so you will see the enormity of the issue, and appreciate the complexity.

How beautiful this is! Imagine the wisdom that may come in the future. Imagine children being born with actual understanding of who they may become, and as soon as they are able to speak and think, they know where they are going. The children will start remembering past experience!

It's time to honor Gaia, even if you live in the city. You can honor Gaia through that which is your consciousness. It's time to honor the ancestry, which is you, and all the things that might have happened in the past. It's time to honor your Akash, which is the relationships that you have with your past lives on this planet. The things that used to be blocks for you are now going to be enhancements for you. Pay attention to your dreams, especially the ones that leave you feeling wonderful and soft-hearted. This is a new energy, only now just beginning to work with you in a different way than before.

"Kryon, you often speak in puzzles and we don't understand what's happening." Take a deep breath. I told you this message would leap around a bit, and be in a circle. So, here's my message:

The three remaining attributes of esoteric relationships will start to develop in the New Human. This is going to enhance awareness and compassion. They will all meld into a balanced Human, and create one who knows that life is all around and is part of the complete picture of everything.

Dear ones, would you please sit down and stop working the puzzle? Just sit and ponder this: Do you understand love? Not really. No Human does. However, can you love? Yes. You can't intellectualize love, so we are telling you to just sit and let some of these things *be*. Let them slowly come into focus, and perhaps you will have what we will call the *aha experience*: *"I know now! I understand it by myself, automatically, because I let go of it."* The best inventions of history have happened when the inventors let go of the puzzle.

The best solutions to problems come when you stop analyzing them. This is the benevolence of Spirit.

The New Human is beginning to awaken on the planet. The children will carry attributes that you did not. However, the Old Soul has the wisdom to begin to use these new attributes in this time on the planet. These are attributes that were not there before.

Expect it all! Expect benevolent change. Awaken with hope that things will be different today and tomorrow for you. Let compassion be your guide. These are the things we speak of and are the things we spoke of earlier. Dear ones, I represent the Creative Source. I'm in love with humanity, and again: Now you know why.

And so it is.

Chapter Three

The Triad

Stand by for a re-write of what we all learned in school about the brain. I always thought my brain was the controller of everything in the body, and also of all my thinking. Kryon invites us to see the relationship with two other attributes in the body that, together, create the balance we have in both health and consciousness. Where does intuition come from? If the brain sends signals to the heart to beat, then why does it continue to keep perfect rhythm for a lifetime, even when the spine is damaged and the signals from the brain are blocked by that spinal damage? The heart continues to beat, as though the signal were still present! What if there is a greater system for us to consider and work with, that gives us a far more complete idea of how we function, or how we think? "The Triad" begins to answer some of these questions.

Lee Carroll

Chapter Three

"The Triad"

Kryon Live Channelling
Given in Charlottesville, Virginia

May 10, 2015

Greetings, dear ones, I am Kryon of Magnetic Service. The pause that always follows the greeting is given for my partner to exit. You might have noticed that there is no seeming preparation for this channelling. In an older energy there would be, where the Human Being has to prepare his mind in such a way that the very structure and the psyche would have to be altered. If you had certain kinds of measurements on his brain, you would see the preparation working. You'd see the various alpha and beta waves change, but not now. The reason is because some time ago, he gave permission for a meld that would mean a continuous connection, a closer walk that would make him a more compassionate Human Being. At the same time, there would be no preparation for channel. He would have one foot in and one foot out of 3D all the time. So when it came time for 100 percent, all he did was step back. But the stepping back is the most difficult thing he does. All of this has to do with the Human brain – what is involved with it that you know about and what you don't know about and what is evolving for you *to now* know about.

The channel tonight is informative and deals with things we have not discussed before in this way. I will be bringing a new concept forward, but it won't be complex, because it's just an introduction. However, it's an introduction to a concept of an evolving humanism.

New is Often Controversial

You are moving forward into a new energy that is going to change the very fabric of your consciousness. I want to explain things that I have never explained before, and some of this will be controversial. Let me comment on this: You believe a certain way because you have learned a certain way. Once you have cognized something [committed belief to it], it actually belongs to you. So what we are saying is that you have a "groove" you have been thinking within for a long time. It's no wonder some of this may hit you the wrong way. But these things can be rewritten if you re-cognize them by choice. So I say to you this: DO NOT take what follows and run with it simply because I said it in channel. I want you to discern this with your own mind and measure it for yourself for viability and common sense. Make it real. Could it be that things are now different than your original training? Did the energy change? If so, is it possible that spiritual awareness has opened more areas of discovery? If you can think out of your "learned box," it may start to actually validate some of the things that you have seen lately. What you originally learned really hasn't changed. It just got bigger and looks different.

The Human Mind is Complex

The Human mind is complex. If you had to compartmentalize it and take a look at the different kinds of thinking that Humans do, it would get even more complex. It has been studied for years, but in a 3D way; the best that you have been able to do is to look at the Human mind as a *succinct operation of synapse that allows survival.* According to your science, the brain gives you everything. It gives you survival; it gives you intuition and mental acuity; it gives you all of your coordinated body functions – everything. You might say that it drives the boat of life.

In addition, when you started studying it more, you discovered that the right and the left lobes do different things and are connected differently between men and women. Everything you studied pointed to the brain being the controller. That was the center of consciousness and all things Human.

The Real Brain Scenario

The concept we bring you this evening is that there is no single brain within the Human Being. Instead, there are three. In order for you to see this clearly in the brief time that we're together, I'm going to give you the best metaphoric illustration I can for what's going on. Under the pretense that you don't know what you don't know, you've done your best. What else could you have done? All you have to look at is the brain! Therefore, the brain is all there is. Come with me and play with this metaphor. It's the best I can do to explain something very special and new.

A Metaphoric Journey

You're in a room, taking a look at a table. It's a workstation, to the modern Human, and on the workstation there is a computer. Almost everyone listening and in this room will recognize the instrument, and many have operated it. Most of you know what it does. However, an Ancient would have no idea. So in this example, and for this metaphoric allegory, we will pretend that we have an Ancient [older one] from only 100 years ago, coming forward to the workstation and being amazed by what he sees.

In this story, you can't communicate with him, but you can show him the computer. So without explanation, without help, and without you being able to say anything, he sees and perceives the magic of what it can do. He can read the screen, and he can interface as he tries to figure out the mouse and the operation of the device. He starts pressing buttons, and he sees things – unbelievable things! This box does things that nobody back home will believe! The future is astonishing! He marvels at the immensity of it all. He discovers Google, but he has no idea of the concept. He sees the world at his fingertips, all in a box. It's heady to think of this power of information and action. There isn't anything it doesn't know! All of the languages of the world are in the box. Any piece of information that he ever wanted to know about anything is in the box! Anything! Then he discovers that you can type a message to just about anyone, anywhere! It's also a communication device!

This is amazing beyond belief, and he eventually walks away from the experience with a solid perception of what he has seen with his own eyes! When he returns in his time machine, he can hardly wait to tell his generation of 100 years ago what he has seen – about technology and a box that does everything and communicates with everyone. It's like all the world's libraries together in a little box – all of the languages, all of the encyclopedias possible and any question you ever wanted to ask. It knows about all of the individuals known throughout history, with all the details – all that is, in the one box – and it's available to every Human Being. The perception, without any explanation, is a solid, logical one, but it's flawed.

The Hidden Connection

You know better, don't you? You see, you know that the "box" is connected to the Internet. If you disconnect the computer from the 'net, it's simply a computational device. It computes. Oh, you may be able to write a letter on it, or you may be able to do a spreadsheet on it, but you can't ask it anything, because it's not connected!

What the Ancient did not understand, nor could he even begin to conceive of, was the World Wide Web. He didn't see the tiny cord that was plugged into the base of the computer, which gave it the magic ability to know everything about everything about everything. Even if he had seen the cord, it would be meaningless to his perception. To him, the box did it all. He had seen it!

Now, let me bring you back to the brain. All you had to examine all these years, as Humans, is what you think is the awesome, magic brain. You don't know about the brain's connection to a multidimensional Internet, which is within the body. How could you?

The Human Brain

Your brain is a large and wonderful chemical, synaptic computer. Let me define this more: Synapse, as we speak of it, is the active process of electromagnetic signals going through neural matrix pathways [structured nerve pathways and bundles] within the brain. It happens from many junction areas [places] to others at lightning speed. It gives you the ability to control your survival, your body and your thoughts in 3D.

Expansive thinking, as you understand it, is brain-related. You've looked at the brain and you've said, *"This is the creative area. It's responsible for music, artwork, poetry, sculpture and the intellect."*

You never saw the wire, did you?

The brain has nothing to do with creating those things. Instead, it facilitates them! It facilitates them, but it isn't responsible for them. Much like the box in the metaphoric room is the control station for the 'net, your brain is the control station for much, much more. These things simply look like they are coming from the box, which is your brain. But they are not.

Much of what you consider creative and/or spiritual, including channelling, is coming from the pineal connection. This includes your intuitive part, which is growing with your spiritual evolution. This is the part of your consciousness that is connected to that which you call the Higher-Self. You can call it what you want, but it's the connection from the Creative Source to the brain. It's there, and some use it well. Some do not. It opens wide only through free choice, and the ones who are creating incredible things are *connected to the 'net* – the pineal. However, you see it as happening within the brain.

The invisible wire that you cannot see, the overlay that you do not recognize within the brain, is the connection to the outside that many of you are beginning to understand and feel. The brain facilitates these attributes, but it does not create them. Intuition does not come from the brain, but it's facilitated by the brain. The brain then activates it into what you call *thought*. You might see it on the graphs of thermography along with all of the things you think are synapses going on in the brain, but the brain is simply processing what it is receiving from somewhere else.

If you unplug the wire to the 'net, all the brain can do for you is to keep you breathing and give you basic survival thinking. You can run from the Bengal tiger so you won't be eaten. You can grow your food, have children, and learn how to drive a car, but it won't write music and it won't create sculpture. It doesn't naturally think of God! It does not analyze itself. But when it's plugged in, it does all that.

The Three Parts – More to Consider Than You Think

There are three parts to the brain of the Human Being, but you are only aware of two of them. We're going to give you the third part tonight. The second brain of the Human Being, which is processed by the synaptical part [the brain box], is the pineal. This is responsible for creative thinking, intuition and intellectual awareness. Intuition is starting to grow with humanity, and it comes from that which is your Innate inside the body. It's getting smarter and is passing more to your brain to process at a greater frequency and strength as you evolve. It also is starting to give you Akashic information [past-life remembrances]. You might say your pineal 'net is getting faster, and your brain is processing it. You are feeling that you are becoming more intuitively aware of things.

The bridge between Human consciousness and the smart body, the Innate, is starting to mature and grow up. You are getting out of pure survival mode and many are starting to awaken to a greater truth. This is all being enhanced in the Human Being to a point where Humans will think, *"The brain is doing better!"* It isn't. The brain remains the brain and will process a better intuition from the pineal. The brain remains a stellar survival organ, but intuition is going to get stronger and stronger. Again, your spiritual Internet is getting faster.

In this very 3D energy, you only see the one organ that you feel is responsible for everything you do, but there are actually three. The evolved Human Being has the potential to create light [awareness energy]. I just gave you something we can study later – information that is new. There's a perception of spirituality being white light. It's everywhere. You've seen it everywhere. There is the story of Moses and the burning bush. This was a flame that did not consume itself, but if you could really see it in reality, it was a white light. For him, it was a higher consciousness than he had ever seen before, an angelic energy coming through his pineal, projecting to him.

When you have a near-death experience, you go to the light. This is more than metaphoric. You start to create something we will call *divinity and mastery*. White light coming from you is the *higher consciousness you.* The more your DNA efficiency is increased, the whiter the light gets. This is a metaphor, but there is truth often behind all mythology, and this is one of those. Dear ones, you are becoming more angelic when you start to understand the third part.

The Third Brain

We have told you before that there is a mystery going on that involves the Human heart. The Human heart, dear ones, is the third part of the brain. Science has never understood why the heart has such a tremendous magnetic field. It is actually larger than any other organ, including the brain with all of its synaptic activity. The heart overshadows it in so many ways, yet examination of the heart in a corporeal way will give information that is seemingly very ordinary. The heart simply pumps blood in a specific rhythm as sent by signals from the brain. Yet there is far more.

When we started, we gave you instructions to *connect the dots,* and here is your chance. When a spinal cord is severed in an accident, the heart continues pumping. Brain signals that supposedly control timing and rhythm are disconnected. The signals are gone, yet the heart keeps pumping. Not only that, but digestion continues, liver function continues, pancreas and others continue, even reproduction continues! All without the brain.

There is a third element of consciousness that is centered within the Human heart. You have identified the heart metaphorically as the symbol of love, and you're right. These three parts to Human consciousness go way beyond the brain as an organ. It's the *trilogy of survival.* It's also represented by the *three* energy [in numerology] that you see everywhere in spiritual history. It's the three horses that pulled the ascension chariot, the Merkabah of Elijah. It's the trilogy Godhead of many churches [Father, Son, Holy Spirit]. In your body, it's the pineal [Creator intuition], the brain [survival] and the heart [compassion].

The masters of this planet had all three working well, but in an older energy, you have not. In an older energy, you were only in survival mode. What is happening is that you are evolving, and the Innate of the body is getting stronger. DNA is starting to become more efficient, and these parts are starting to finally connect. Dear ones, what separates a Human Being in survival from a master is *intuitive compassion*. Compassion is generated from the heart and it's not a metaphor. It is part of the heart-brain.

There are things going on in this trilogy that you should understand. Connect the dots and start using science to find out and recognize that there are things that are not visible in any spectrum you can yet measure. But simply because you are blind to it at the moment doesn't mean it's not happening. You simply have not discovered everything yet, but the advancement in multidimensional physics will help. Listen, as new physics inventions come to you, you must involve biology, too! Don't separate the two sciences [as they are now]. You will have a far better idea of the truth of all of this when you can quantum-map emotion, thinking and Human behavior. It will show itself immediately.

The brain is responsible for facilitating [coordinating] all three of these parts, but be aware that the other two are doing a great deal of the work. Intuition and compassion will always seem to come directly from the brain, just like to the Ancient when the magic came from the box. Connect yourself to a bigger picture, dear ones. The triad of Human consciousness is the beginning of the realization of mastery.

That's all we want to tell you now. It's something for you to digest into your logic and spirituality, is it not? Think about it and ask your own intuition, *"Is it true? Could it be that the Human brain is only a facilitator for something bigger?"* This information starts to explain some measurements you never could explain before with conventional biological beliefs. It starts to explain why it is when a Human Being makes certain kinds of decisions, suddenly the brain seems to control the body better. Why is it that corporeal health can suddenly change, heal itself, ask for other kinds of foods, and have biological wisdom? What causes spontaneous remission? Dear ones, unless you were connected, you wouldn't have any of this. Think: It isn't the brain that gave any of that to you. It was the brain that simply facilitated the connection from that little wire – the Creative Source, the white light.

There have been metaphors given tonight and things for you to examine, which also mean other things. It is the way that we begin the teaching of profound things. We will do it again and again, then elaborate on and on, and talk endlessly about it – all so that you will get it. It's time you knew the grander picture of the triad, the trilogy of creation inside the Human Being.

I am Kryon, in love with humanity and for good reason.

And so it is.

"Humanity is going to start living longer for a number of reasons. There will come a day when quantum energy can be used for amazing life extension and healing. This will be artificial activation with other fields that are quantum, and partial rejuvenation will be the result."

Kryon

Chapter Four

The Future of DNA

Here we are again, mixing chemistry with esoterics. Some people continue to ask, *"What does my DNA have to do with my spirituality?"* God is the master physicist and biologist, and has created it all with perfect elegance and harmony. Everything we have is integrated with everything else on the planet. All the life-chemistry in your body is part of your spirituality, and responds to your very consciousness. Kryon Book Ten even designates the twelve esoteric layers of DNA as the twelve names of God. Your Akashic Record is in your DNA, as well as the very seeds of the Creator (God Inside). This has been the theme of Kryon for many years: Our DNA is the blueprint for our very awareness, and will start to evolve in certain ways, to give us an entirely different paradigm of living, in the future. It's not just chemistry. There is some science presented here, but mostly, it's an explanation of what DNA is going to provide for the New Human, as we continue to evolve.

Do you believe in "Genesis Cells"? This concept is presented here first, but then it continues into the chapter after this one as well.

Lee Carroll

Chapter Four

"The Future of DNA"

Kryon Live Channelling
Given in Minneapolis, Minnesota

August 1, 2015

Greetings, dear ones, I am Kryon of Magnetic Service. My partner steps aside, as he must for a channel like this to be given. He knows what this is like and has done it many times. He's in a place, if you wish to call it that, and he is listening like you are listening. He has distractions, however, that are not the ones that you have, and he has spoken of this before.

He is not talking now. I am and, again, we say that perception must be clean for you in order to cognize what is being said. I speak of things that are beyond his knowledge and I talk about the real energy of this planet that is physical right now. We've spoken of odd physics many times, but we're not going to today. Instead, we're going to talk about physical, three-dimensional things that are affecting you through a multidimensional source that is changing that which you know and understand.

Planetary Shift Has Been The Prophecy of Many

We have said now for years that physical change was coming to the planet. The prophecies have been clear in their own vague way, and they say that the consciousness of the planet itself is going to shift, and that the planet will become "softer" in humanism, and that unexpected things would happen. We even told you there might be a *wild card* coming and that you're going to get more of them. These wild cards would be unexpected or improbable things – world-changing inventions you didn't expect, actions from others you didn't expect and even benevolence you didn't expect. Softer energy is coming to you, and that is very sweet, and many have said that's a good prediction and a wonderful prophecy. I want to tell you what's really happening, however, and I want to give you the ABCs of it, as you say. I want to give you the physical 3D reality of what's going on around you.

Some of this will appear to you as a review, but it isn't. It's a consolidation of many little pieces that I have given you before, in order to show you what is going on today. The subject is DNA. DNA is not simply a chemical molecule in your body. It is a multidimensional piece of divinity. The very molecule that you call DNA is all over the galaxy, dear ones. It is life and it is the way life forms everywhere. It is the patterning and the geometry of life everywhere and you're going to see this someday, as you are able to examine other life you find outside your planet. DNA can only change through physics, for it is physics that controls chemistry. It's about to change.

The Physics of Consciousness

Let me review some things I have said in the past, so you can see how it relates to the lesson today. Twenty-six years ago, when I started giving messages, I told my partner to write in his first book, that the magnetic grid of the Earth would be shifting. Indeed, it did. This is now science history, and magnetic north moved a few degrees since that time. I gave the message that your magnetic grid is related to, or intertwined with, the *physics of Human consciousness*. Be clear on this: Consciousness is not a wispy esoteric thing that can't be measured. It's real physics that you just have not seen yet. Many experiments on the planet at this moment are aware that the strength of the magnetic field actually shifts with mass Human consciousness [a coherence with compassionate events on the planet]. When you are eventually able to measure multidimensional fields in a clearer way, you will be able to see the correlation between the magnetic field of the Earth and Human consciousness. Therefore, you might say, *"As goes the grid goes Human consciousness."* Now you know why I'm called, "The Magnetic Master."

The Magnetic Grid and The Change Coming

What you should be aware of is that the grid hasn't moved much in Human history and has remained fairly static through your many lifetimes. In 1987, however, it started to move a lot. The reason? It is moving so it can be positioned to receive something – something expected that is coming. Think of it as moving your furniture so that you can better view something you didn't know was viewable. The reposturing of the grid is for something coming that we are going to call "evolutionary energy" and it's physical. It is really physical! In fact, you can even see it coming!

Months ago and years before that, we told you that your planet is going into an area of space that it never has been in before. This is not esoteric. Ask an astronomer, *"Is the solar system coming out of a protective bubble into a new kind of radiation or energy that you haven't seen before?"* Is it possible that your solar system is losing a protective sheath that it's always had because of where it was in space?

Let me explain this more to those who don't understand much about galactic movement and your solar system. All the stars in your galaxy are slowly moving around the center. Your solar system and its star [the Sun] has always been on the move as it rotates around the center of the galaxy. As your solar system rotates around the middle, you are always in a new period of time and space. It moves so slowly, however [millions of years to go around one time], that for all of humanity, it has basically been in one energy, like a protective bubble – and now it changes. Don't believe it? Do your research or ask an astronomer if there is something different. Make this channelling real to you, and you will understand more fully what we are saying to you.[1]

The Role of the Sun

As you move into this new energy, or what some have even called "radiation," you should know how it works, for it's very related to your Sun. Physically, it affects the magnetic field of the Sun [the heliosphere], which then in turn is blasted to your own [Earth's] magnetic field via the solar wind. That's the physics of it, but dear ones, let me give you the esoterics of it. This has been the plan all along, that if you made it as a Human race past the 2012 marker, you would pass into this area of space and the magnetics would shift, allowing Human consciousness to change. Dear ones, this was always here waiting for you to pass the marker! This is why I came 26 years ago and told you the magnetics would shift. This is an evolutionary energy that is going to affect your Sun – the heliosphere of your Sun – which then will pass to the magnetic field of the Earth, a field that has now been repostured for this new consciousness.

Oh, there are those intellectuals who would say, *"Well, what if we had destroyed ourselves as the prophecies said we would? What if there were no Humans to receive this?"* It's simple. No Humans would have been here, but the planet would have still moved into this new area of space and the same energies would have been there, but you would not have been. Simple. But indeed, here you are!

So now you can see that the prophecy from the indigenous is also being fulfilled, for they told you about the changes coming after the precession of the equinoxes [December 2012]. How could they have had this prophecy about your movement into a new place around your galaxy? Think about it! These things are not new, and even the Ancients told you it was coming! They may not have known the specifics of science, but their prophecy is the same one I have: New consciousness is coming.

Dear ones, I want you to continue to put together these pieces physically in what you can see. As we told you, these changes affect your Sun. The heliosphere of your Sun changes your magnetic grid. Now, for this all to work, the Sun had to be *quiet* for this. I want you to ask an astronomer about the Sun and the cycles of the Sun. Ask about what period of radiance the Sun is in at the moment. The astronomer will tell you that it appears to be one of the quietest cycles that the Sun has ever seen. Solar flares and sunspots are disturbances in the multidimensional field that surrounds the Sun, so these had to be gone while the new energies were starting to be implemented. For this all to work, the Sun had to be as quiet as possible, and it is. The Sun's quiet time is also affecting your weather, and we told you that, too. Due to its quietness, you're in a cycle of weather that we also predicted [a cold time coming] that also has a lot to do with the energy that's coming. That's physical. Ask an astronomer, *"Are they worried about all this?"* Some of them are and others are not. But it is affecting you and the planet right now. Now you know why the magnetic grid was changed when it was changed and why. That's physical.

The Esoterics of It All

Now, at the same time that all this [magnetic] physical shift was happening, we gave you esoteric information about the Pleiadian *nodes and the nulls.*[2] Is it possible that the Pleiadians themselves, having been here at the beginning and knowing about this coming change, actually helped with the prophecies [influenced the ancient calendars and prophecies]? Indeed, this is true, but it appeared to the indigenous as "intuition from the ancestors." The nodes and the nulls left by the Pleiadians are fast-track engines that are affect-

2   www.kryon.com/80-2

Chapter Four   81

ing the grids of the planet.[3] Consciousness is related to the grids of the planet, remember? But not just the Magnetic Grid was involved. It also includes the Crystalline Grid [Human emotional remembrance] and the Gaia grids – all of them. These are all being worked on at this time in combination with the new evolutionary energy from the Sun. These grids are being fed, if you want to call it that, by the nodes and the nulls. What is it all doing? What is the real bottom line of all this? The answer: These confluences of energies that are shifting and changing are all directly affecting one thing – your DNA.

The DNA Evolution is Coming

The DNA of the Human Being is ready to shift and change. You'll never see it in a microscope, because it's not chemical; it's physics. Listen for a moment, for you have already seen how this works. The 90 percent of DNA that heretofore was junk is now understood by your science.[4] Science now understands that this 90 percent is information – a manual – a control panel for the genes. But it's still a mystery as to what it actually contains or how it gives out the information to the genes. What is not acknowledged yet is that it is a multidimensional transmission. To most biologists that would be a stretch, but there actually is a bit of quantumness in your DNA, and this has also been scientifically seen (Gariaev and Poponin experiments with DNA).[5]

This 90 percent of DNA is like trillions of antennas in your body, ready to receive information and then rewrite the manual via the changes in your grids. The DNA is going to receive information and shift. It's going to affect genetics. Mothers will receive it first and pass it to their children. Mothers, you don't even know you've got it, yet you are passing it to your kids right now. Are you aware

---

3   www.kryon.com/81-3
4   www.kryon.com/81-4
5   www.kryon.com/81-5

of the books of my partner from more than 10 years ago about "The Indigo Children"? These children were precursors to the new energy. The kids are different! It started before 2012 – way before – since the potentials were very high that you would make it, and you did. Mothers of grandchildren, do I have to ask you if they are different? Very different!

Changes in the Kids are First

A Human baby comes into the planet today, but what is going on today is different from when you were born. You're in a new place in space, the Sun is quiet, you have the nodes and the nulls feeding new information into the grids, and the paradigm of consciousness is different for them than it was for you. Their Genesis cells, the "how a Human works" cells, are changing.

Things will start working that are unusually different for standard Human nature. The intuitive self, the barrier between Innate and consciousness, will start to improve. The barrier starts to become less. Be ready for children who have very accurate intuition about what's wrong with them. If they tell you something's wrong, take them to the doctor! Immediately. Don't tell them, *"It's your imagination, honey,"* or, *"It will be okay later; it's growing pains."* Do you hear that? There are those listening to this right now who need to hear that, because their children are saying, *"I feel funny; something's wrong."* Mothers who are used to raising children are also used to an old energy paradigm that has a certain *health template*. This is changing. The kids are starting to awaken to being intuitive about their own health. The bridge isn't built yet to Innate, but it is closer with them and they're *feeling* something. Innate is talking to them for the first time. Listen: You didn't have it, but they do. Listen to them.

The Akash of the child is starting to become clearer. These children are going to tell you many things about who they've been and what they've done. If you're a parent and you are listening to this now, the worst thing you can do is suppress it. The best thing you can do is to tell the child the absolute truth, the absolute truth: *"I believe you."* When you say things out loud, it helps the child. That's truthful and the child will get it. Listen, parent: In these things, be an ally to your child, and it will change your relationship with your children. Be honest with them about it all. Tell them, not everyone will understand, so there are times to be quiet about it. These are instructions for kids in the New Age. These attributes are going to get even stronger, and your instructions will make sense.

Instinct is going to work better than it ever has. Instinct is not something that you are used to seeing much in Humans. You see it in animals mostly, because the offspring of animals have a very strong survival instinct. It is passed to them so well that they can actually walk within hours of birth! You don't have that. However, this same mechanical passing of instinct is starting to become stronger in Humans, and especially that which will come from the Akash. It is chemical as well as being esoteric [genetic and Akashic]. As it is in animals, you should have it also and you will. You're going to see children remembering how to walk and how to eat much earlier, without training. It will be faster than the older paradigm, and faster than the doctors who know about child development will have seen. It will be "off the scale." Get ready for it; it's instinct. It's simple chemistry. It's the DNA working better.

If you look at the DNA [in the] cell itself, you might ask, what is happening? The truth is that DNA is becoming more informed, some say, "enabled." Now, there is a buzzword in esoteric belief called *activation*. Please don't change it, but know that it's not ac-curate. You are not activating anything. Instead, you are releasing DNA from a prison. If you have somebody who is crippled in a chair, shriveled and not able to move, yet suddenly they are released from this bondage, and the fingers untangle and the hand starts to become whole again, it's because something has happened to the DNA. It hasn't happened to the hand, or to the muscle, or to the fingers, not even to the arm, but to the DNA. It's a *release*. I want you to hold this vision. All the changes I have talked about are about being released from a prison of crippled DNA! And – get ready – it happens to ALL DNA in the body at once. It's a "whole body experience," not a local "hand/arm" one.

Your DNA is crippled in this old energy, and it's your own free choice that created this. Your DNA, your lifespan [aging], your diseases are all where you wanted to take the energy of this planet, and your DNA cooperated. This is what you've lived with, and what is now changing. It's not DNA activation, it's DNA release. Release!

The profundity of it all: Do you realize the help that you have? Did you think for a moment that all of this was going to be *you* just doing these things? It involves the galaxy, the part of space you're in, the nodes and the nulls, and the Creator of the Universe. It involves the Pleiadians; it involves your timeline; and it involves love. All of this is for you to sit in a new energy and release the bonds of your DNA. Now, dear ones, old souls, there is something you ought to know. You don't have to wait to be reborn for this. The old soul has the equipment inside right now, just like the newborn.

DNA Templates

Your DNA is filled with information and *templates*. Now, templates are patterns and paradigms of life. Most of these templates are ones you have that are not complete. Now, what you don't know about a template is that it has what we would call a patterning of its own. If you have a portion of a template already, that is to say, *a piece of the design*, it draws to itself the rest of the design, if it can. Did you understand that? If you have a piece of the picture, that piece has an attitude – an attitude of desire – wanting the rest of the picture! As soon as it's possible to get that missing piece, it's like magnetics. It literally flies to itself and the template snaps into place and you get the whole thing. All of you have pieces of the template and the ones who have the most profoundly "ready" pieces are old souls [the ones reading this]. Your Earth experience has waited for this! You are then going to complete the templates that are missing, old soul.

Genesis Cells: The Starting Template

This term I'm using in this message is a Kryon term today, not a medical term. There may be a medical term similar, but this is different. One of the templates that always exists and never goes away is part of the *Human manual*. It's not as linear as in this explanation, but it will work. Think of it this way: I want you to think of the *manual of birth*. When you came in, what was the manual like? What page were you on when you were five days old? What page were you on at six months? What page were you on when you were 30? You all know that all the pages are different because of the chronology of growing up.

The pages are still there, and the template is still there for what I call Genesis cells. Genesis cells, as I will define them, are the cells of a newborn that accelerate growth and learning in a special way. The child absorbs so much of the world around him/her in six months. This includes speech, language, the beginning of standing and walking, and much more. The antennas of the Genesis manual are so big! They are listening to the attitudes and the consciousness of everything around them. You already know that. It's active for a newborn Human, then it slows down and you become the adult. Genesis cells are magic. They are used at first, then they are not, but they're still there and never go away. The template is still there, the instruction sets for how they are made, if you want to call it that, are still there. This is all physics, for the chemistry of how it all works is physics. What you should know about the children of today is that the *antennas* are up to 10 times as long as they were for you.

Now, old soul, what if I told you that you could release these cells now, make them active for you? They could be available for you now, just go get them in the manual. Do it with affirmations, do it with consciousness change, do it with meditation. However you communicate with Innate, it's ready to release the Genesis cells from their time prison to be used again! What that means to you is fast-track growth to enlightenment! They work with the Akash!

It's for any situation you might have. Don't limit it to what you *think* you need! Always ask, *"Dear Spirit, what do I need?"* State, *"Dear Spirit, this and something better."* Use this potential! Genesis cells are ready for the old soul. I keep saying *old soul,* did you notice? In other words, a number of lifetimes gives you the template information that a newbie would not have who has only been on the Earth a few times. Old souls have hundreds of lifetimes, maybe thousands, in order to develop experience and the template of knowledge. Every one of you in this room can say to yourself, *"I know that I've been here before,"* and your Innate will vibrate with the truth of it. You know too much! You feel too much! You're in this room listening to channelling! This message is accurate and it's true. You're an old soul. Everything I've just told you is about the enhancement of the Human Being in an energy that you have expected.

I close with this: The secret to mining your Akash, or releasing the template, is by having a compassionate consciousness. Does that surprise you? That's what has been missing all along. If you are going to mine your Akash [pull upon the things you have learned in the past] and start rewriting who you are, you're going to have to come to an agreement of compassion with yourself. How are you doing with lack of anger, care for others, purity of God inside? The physics of consciousness to create compassion creates what I call *compassionate action.* It's for everyone in the room and those reading. An old soul knows how to do this. Listen: I know who you are. You wouldn't be listening or reading unless you were an old soul. You are one, and you know you are. Compassion is the king of all emotions at this point on the planet. It's going to lead you into an evolved state of love, and without compassion and caring for others, it is not going to work. In fact, nothing will work.

Very slowly there is going to be a split of consciousness on the planet, and we have talked to you about it before. There will be those who are compassionate and those who are not, and it's going to be obvious, so obvious! Caring and uncaring. There is a dark army right now on this planet. What is its "compassion factor"? Do you understand? It's a free choice state of mind, but that's the split to come. Don't worry about this, compassionate one. When you take the attributes of the master, light surrounds you. No more fortressing or protecting yourself from darkness. It will retreat from you automatically. No more catching the diseases of the day, they won't be able to touch you with compassion. It's physics; it's real; it's physical; and it's happening now. Your society will reflect this sooner than you think. When you turn on your news and you think I'm crazy, just wait. There's some wild cards coming. Benevolence is a new energy!

I'm Kryon, in love with humanity.

And so it is.

TRUTH IS WHAT YOU MAKE OF IT – KRYON AND THE JEWS

On page 81 is an Internet reference[6] to the excellent science of Dr. Vladimir Poponin and Dr. Peter Gariaev. It shows that DNA may actually have a field or a multidimensional component. I always like to include good science links whenever possible, to enhance the validity of what Kryon is saying, which many would never know

---

about otherwise. These men are also referenced by some of my author friends in metaphysics.

However, I am always amazed at the fact that good science in a metaphysical channelling book is simply not acceptable to some. Here is an anonymous ("prof 77") blog entry prefacing another related science page[7], which refers to these two fine scientists:

Note: Unfortunately, a supposed "angelic" trance channelled entity 'Kryon' cited this article (August 1, 2015). I stand by the article below. However, I do not consent to and I do not associate with Kryon in any way and, in fact, I feel Kryon is a racist who attempts to divide us against each other. Specifically, Kryon says one race is superior to all others: "Kryon's message is that Jews are a special group amongst humans, "a pure karmic group", the chosen people." (Source: https://en.wikipedia. org/wiki/Lee_Carroll) Yikes! Sorry about that. Now, on to the article…

Although the blog is anonymous, my feeling is that it, indeed, may be an associate of said scientists, or a teacher of the science, since there seems to be a feeling of "ownership" of the science stated within the blog. Also note the reference to Wikipedia. Please! Wikipedia is misinformation, and can't be altered, even by the person Wikipedia is writing about! See my warning here[8]. The Wikipedia page for Kryon, Lee Carroll, and The Indigo Children is packed with blatantly wrong and misleading information. My attempts to correct it, for over a decade, have had no results. Wikipedia is purposely biased in many subjects, and even teachers refuse to use it in mainstream education. I hope you never are listed on Wikipedia, since whatever it says to millions on Earth is exactly what a few want to say, not what is accurate – and there is no way you can correct it effectively.

I'm used to people not understanding channelling, in fact, I didn't either! Through most of my life, I made fun of it (referring

---

7   www.kryon.com/88-7
8   www.kryon.com/88-8

to it as the "lunatic fringe"), so there is absolutely no issue from me with anyone saying that Kryon is fake, or rolling their eyes at the idea of it all. That's standard. However, it's really interesting to watch people's reaction to Kryon, when he speaks of the Jews.

I have lost friends and followers, simply because of a phrase that Kryon used, without them ever examining what Kryon meant. It seems ingrained in some to have a "knee jerk" reaction to some subjects, and this is one of them. They hear one phrase, then slam the door to anything else that is being said or explained. It speaks multitudes about people's feelings, and the subject of the Jews and the Middle East – and the biases of many, including those who chose to define Kryon incorrectly on Wikipedia and keep it that way.

Kryon has been giving information about the Jewish lineage for over twenty years. He also told us yet again in this book (The Israel channellings) that the Jews are "chosen people." (Pages 166-169.) This phrase is heard, or read, and, for whatever reason, people immediately slam the book shut, or quit coming to Kryon seminars, or call Kryon a racist. Sadly, all of the above has happened, without ever listening or reading further to what Kryon means by that phrase.

Setting the record straight, yet again: The Jews are the CHOSEN ones *to accomplish a giant responsibility*: They are CHOSEN for two things: (1) To bring monotheism to the planet (which they did), and (2) To bring peace to the Middle East (which is still in progress). They are more "tasked" than chosen. The idea that Kryon would elevate one kind of people above another is the most un-Kryon thing imaginable! Anyone who has studied the channellings of Kryon knows this. The Jews are not CHOSEN as an elitist group. Hardly! The "pure Jewish Akashic lineage" that Kryon speaks of is simply a spiritual mechanism so their DNA won't get "watered down" genetically through thousands of years. The reason for this is to accomplish the challenging task they are here for: The eventual settling of the most difficult peace puzzle we have on the planet – Peace in Israel. They are CHOSEN to work it out!

Kryon channelled this exact message at the Habima Theater in Tel Aviv on October 8, 2015, to a sold-out audience – mostly Israelis.[9]

Blessings to all of you!

Lee Carroll

Chapter Five

The Hidden Youth Template

For a very long time, science has wondered if the body retains the original blueprint (when you were conceived) that creates a Human Being from a tiny embryo. Could it be, that this blueprint actually still exists within us? Kryon says it does, and that science will find it soon. He even labelled it in a previous channelling "The Genesis Cell." However, can we use this "Youth Template" now? Is this too odd to be true? Why should it still exist? Isn't the body done with it? Kryon asks: When you build something really exceptional, do you throw away the blueprints? Even if it's only built once, do you toss the plans that made it? The answer is no. There are really good reasons to keep the blueprint of original Human development. Part of this is exactly what this channel speaks of: We need it to repair and rejuvenate the New Human in a new energy.

Lee Carroll

Chapter Five

"The Hidden Youth Template"

Kryon Live Channelling
Given in San Rafael, California

December 12, 2015

Greetings, dear ones, I am Kryon of Magnetic Service. My partner, I wish you to go slow and measure the words. Make sure the information is correct as it is given. This is the next to the last channel of 2015, and it's time to bring you more information for your future.

Some will say that this is a science channel, but it really isn't. If you are listening later, or reading, then you're listening in the future, as many see it now in the room. However, you don't think of it as the future, because for you, it's now. For me it's now also, but this channelling was really given in your past. For the crowd in front of me, it's now. How do you like it so far? Whose now is real? The answer is, that they all are. We speak to many of you outside of the time frame that you think is yours, but the information is for all the nows. When you hear a wonderful tune sung by one who has passed, or perhaps it was written by someone who is also no longer here, does it then diminish the tune? NO. The music is forever, and the emotions and excitement from hearing it is in all nows. It remains fresh and fun.

This channel may be brought forward later, and presented in a venue you don't expect, in order to discuss something you've just discovered (in a coming future), or to validate what you now realize is true. However, when this channelling was given, the things discussed were not yet there. Confused yet? It's that kind of a channel today. My partner gets chills, for he knows that this information is beautiful and it's appropriate for its time. He knows it's desired and that humanity wants what is coming now. So he goes slow.

I want to talk about a discovery. It's a coming discovery and like many, it happens gradually, with other discoveries that will precede it. Before I discuss what it is or how it works, I want to give you some things to think about. Question: Is it possible that there is a template existing in your DNA that carries the secret of your youth? It would be a template that isn't simply stored data somewhere, but instead, is part of the molecular structure of multi-dimensional DNA, which could be activated or exposed by certain processes. If that were to happen, it could then change everything about the Human Being to whom it belongs. Is it possible that there is something inside every single DNA molecule, and other specific biology within you, which could keep you alive two, three, four times as long as you're living now?

Is there a template of birth – a design that can become [manifest into] profound chemistry, but that is simply laying there now as an inactive instruction set? If so, it's outside of the purview of your three-dimensional thinking about DNA and how it works. It would be very difficult to justify the idea within the existing thinking of the day, and because of how science feels about these kinds of things.

What do you think about the prophets who lived 900 years? I jump right to it. I want you to answer the question inside. If you're a scientist or a skeptic, go ahead and answer it. Foolishness? A "typo" in scripture? It was reported in many ways and in many places and from different sources: Some of the characters you read about in the scriptures or the history books lived far longer than any other Human Beings have ever lived.

Number one: Is it actually possible? If so, how?

Number two: Would there be some kind of spiritual reasoning for that to occur?

Number one: Is it possible? I am sitting here in the chair telling you that it is not only possible, but it was done in certain cases with certain Human Beings in history.

Number two: It was done with the males only, and they lived grand lifetimes for the procreation of the race, and to promote their consciousness. It is simple mechanics. The male seed is fertile to the end. Females are not, and the eggs have chemistry that is age-related. It was the man who had to live a very, very long time in order to pass the seed through many, many children into a fresh area of the planet, which needed that consciousness. Now you know why.

So, what was the process to keep these special men alive for that duration? How? It's simple: They had an activated template of youth. Now, I'm using terminology that is not medical, not scientific, but accurate and true. Listen: Right now, there is actually terminology that exists for this – a name for it, because it's suspected in biology – more than suspected – it's expected. This means that science has seen the "shadow" of it for years. This means that they know it's there, but not much more.

When a Human Being has spontaneous remission, or what some have called spontaneous healing, what exactly occurs? You can't sit there and deny this happens, for it's very real. Do you believe it? You have to, for current science has seen it. It has been reported and documented. So the big question becomes: How did it work? This has always been the mystery of the ages.

There are those who believe that the consciousness of the individual who is sick, somehow brings it about. That's correct – totally correct. Remember that. That is why they call it spontaneous. It wasn't expected, and there was no indication it was coming. This would mean that through consciousness alone, and perhaps without even knowing it, there was an activation of the template. It healed so fast and in such an amazing way, that it was beyond that which was recognizable as possible in current medical belief or understanding.

It's almost like the body cleaned itself of the disease. It took it out, and even removed the markers that showed the disease had ever been there! It means that cellular rejuvenation was accelerated greatly for a few days, or a few weeks, to clean out that which did not belong there, and it saved the life of the individual.

Spontaneous, automatic remission of a disease is real, and comes from a place in the biology that is in every single person. Human logic is often funny: There are those who say, "*Ah, it's the Placebo Effect! That's all it is.*" Okay, what is the Placebo Effect? The Placebo Effect is human consciousness creating healing results through expectation. There you are! In the Placebo Effect, you have consciousness ruling the chemistry of the body, and that's exactly what we are telling you: Full and complete expectation of healing, activates the template. With DNA working at only about 30 percent (in your existing energy), the Placebo Effect is just an anomaly of a greater process of the Youth Template. It's something that is actually showing itself, so you can believe it's possible.

Let's talk about a little science. There is an area of physics called quantum. It is the study of alternate realities created by particles in a quantum field. Related to this, you also have something called quantum biology. It is a real science discipline, and the premise is this: Biology, which intrinsically has physics, then also has quantum areas. Therefore, the molecule of DNA itself, or perhaps any other molecule, must have some quantum attributes, as well as three-dimensional attributes. Now, for whatever reason, this is controversial. You expect quantum attributes in physics, yet somehow, there is a wall, a barrier, when you talk about biology! It's as though biology had no physics! In fact, biology primarily is physics. For, chemistry depends upon the very things that quantumness depend on.

The spin of electrons around the atoms that come together to create certain combinations in the chemistry of life, are as susceptible to being affected by a quantum field as any other electrons. In fact, the effect is more profound in a life science than one that is not [non-life science based]. Question: What have the quantum biologists discovered? They've discovered that some quantum energies actually change DNA in interesting ways. They don't know why, but when DNA is placed within quantum energy experiments, it changes the spin of the electrons in the quantum field. Listen: Forget the science talk. Know this: DNA has quantum attributes! Period. So does Human Consciousness. Connect the dots.

Doctors, let me talk to you: There is a suspicion that within certain molecules there are things that should be able to be seen, but so far they are elusive. The results are there in experiments, but you cannot see what is "doing the work," even through an electron microscope. You say, these things must exist, for the result of the experiments wouldn't be as they are, but they are "invisible," or perhaps not where they are expected to be. The truth is that they are partially quantum, and have some multidimensional attributes. This means that they can "move around" in odd ways, similar to light.

So they're not invisible, they're just slightly multidimensional. This then, carries us into our next discussion: This beautiful body template that we are discussing, which exists in many molecules, including DNA, is only visible if it is exposed by another multidimensional force. Let's say it again in different words, my partner. Here it comes again: The suspected quantum template energy in certain molecules will show itself [become active] only when exposed to other quantum energies. Period. This is a premise, dear ones, that you need to study. You need quantum energies to activate, energize, and study other quantum energies. They will only "wake up" when exposed to other multidimensional energies.

So, if you could "see" it, what would it look like? The non-scientific answer is this: It will have cluster patterns. These are patterns that you may not recognize, because you have not seen it yet in a three-dimensional biology. However, you've always suspected it would be there. Let's call it what you think it is: It's the Youth cluster, or the Youth (patterned) Template. When certain experiments are done, it starts to show itself for a moment, and then it's gone.

Some have applied magnetics as the multidimensional force, to expose the template. The experiment goes like this: You take the mixture of chemistry and you expose it to a magnetic field. Then you take a look at it the best you can with an electronic microscope. You look for what you suspected was there, and lo and behold – you see a piece of it. It's there! How many years ago did we tell you about magnetics? How many years ago did we tell you that magnetics is needed for life and is a profound part of biology? However, it's only when you create and use what we call designer magnetics (custom designed magnetic fields), that it will reveal what you are looking for, but not with an ordinary magnet. A magnet is not good enough. It's not elegant at all. It's like the difference between "sound in the air" and "language in the air." The language is "elegant sound."

So the discovery? You're going to come up with a far better and more sophisticated, designed quantum energy, to make quantum things vibrate in a way that they are visible or become activated. Magnetism qualifies as a source, but not unless it's a designed magnetic field. A multidimensional force will reveal the template's attributes. The template itself represents everything biological in your body. Most of the reason is because it's part of the programming of the DNA. Spontaneous remission is the template being activated. In most cases, you have seen it being done by the Human's consciousness, It's either survival or death, and each Human has their process. Most often, the process is fear, and you've seen it over and over. However, occasionally an old soul is faced with this, and the template "kicks in" and you get to see what the body was designed to do. That should give you chills, dear ones.

The Future

One of the things that's going to happen in biology is the increase in the acknowledgement of the quantumness of cellular structure, and a beginning study of the possibility of a multidimensional life force in every Human Being. This is not what is being studied today. Only the chemistry is being studied today, and the results are obvious: Chemistry (drugs) are medicine's only answer to body issues. If the body is a chemical system, then chemicals will shape it, repair it, and heal it. This was good logic for an older time, but now things are beginning to change. When stimulated correctly, the Youth Template will show itself. Then things will start to change forever in medicine. The "New Human" will be one that medicine sees as a quantum biological machine, and energy – not chemistry – will be the way of all healing – and consciousness is energy!

Now, let's turn the page. Scientists, it was nice to have you here. But now you can stop reading, because we are going to talk about things that you will say are eye-rolling to the max. You'll say, "*It couldn't be this way! It just isn't the way things work.*" But it is, and now I reveal what Innate really is.

The Smart Body, that which you have called Innate, is in total control of the exposure or activation of the Youth Template. When multidimensional forces are applied, Innate sees this and activates what it should activate. Innate is totally responsible for the success of homeopathy. In this, a tincture (remedy), far too small to have a chemical reaction, is placed under the tongue. It "signals" Innate for what the Human wants, and the healing begins. So, you might ask, "*Where is the multidimensional energy-force in homeopathy?*" It's interesting, is it not, that if a Human doesn't believe that homeopathy works, the results are often very limited. The multidimensional energy is belief! Societies all over the planet have believed in it and have been using it very successfully for centuries. The Smart Body is also the one that can be "muscle tested" for answers to biological questions, for which your consciousness has no answers. This science is called Kinesiology. Innate is the Smart Body Intelligence that has no biological source that you would recognize as a source. Innate does NOT come from your brain. Innate is not a brain function.

The brain is a computer that is built for survival, and it works very well. You do something, and it remembers it. If you hurt yourself from some action, you don't do that action again. You have experiences in the past, that help you survive moment to moment in the present. Your remembering function is in your brain, and your brain gives you existence perception, logic, moral direction, and is the central control of most body functions. It's a great organ. The creative things that you do (music, art, writing, spirituality) come from your pineal. We have told you this before. The consciousness that goes beyond the brain and the pineal, makes up The Triad (which we have mentioned before) and that includes the heart.

The heart is so important! It actually doesn't just pump blood. It is involved in some of the things that scientists say the brain is doing, but it's the heart that's doing it. There are those who would say, "*Kryon, we scientifically know that there are no brain functions in the heart.*" Oh – but there are! There's synapse in the heart, if you want to look for it, for the heart is connected to the whole body in ways that have not yet been acknowledged by the mainstream. There is also a great amount of magnetism in the heart, if you want to look for it. It's far more than you think, and there are all manner of things related to the heart that are "brain-like." However, the heart is not Innate. So what is Innate? How does it work and what's going to happen?

We've talked in the past about the future of humanity starting to change. This change is mostly in consciousness, but since consciousness is a whole-body experience, it involves the new Humans who are arriving. So it's going to be seen first in children being born with a much more advanced Innate. In other words, the ability to tie together that which you've experienced the last lifetime and this lifetime, will be enhanced. What this means is that you don't make the same mistakes again in the next life! That is an enhanced Innate. I still haven't told you where it comes from, have I? Oh, I will.

A child burns his finger on a stove, then he never touches a stove for the rest of his life. That's a great brain function, isn't it? Did the Innate have anything to do with it? Indeed! You see, the Innate is the Smart Body, agreeing with the brain. It's all integrated. Now, listen to this: here is what the Innate is going to do with a newborn: The newborn will not touch a stove either, because the newborn remembers from the last lifetime what it's like. So you might say, he carries it over from the past, and you're going to call it instinct. Instinct is much like what the animals have – inherited remembrance. Don't touch the stove. Humans are going to start having that (finally), but next is where inherited instinct stops, and Innate begins.

The newborn is also going to sense, intuitively, the mistakes that were made in his immediate past life, which caused emotional distress, drama, fear, and dysfunction – and then not do them again! The newborn is going to carry in the wisdom from the past life of mistakes made. Part of that whole "mistake scenario" is always physical and emotional. So you might say, it relates to the brain as well. Indeed, it's the Innate that will tie these all together and help the newborn remember it all in an intuitive way, and pass it forward intact.

Now I'm going to tell you what Innate is, and this is often confusing, because you will tend to always linearize it. You will not be able to understand how this passes from one life to another, because you don't know how multidimensional things work, especially when it has to do with the soul. Innate is not the soul, but it knows the soul.

There's a Hebrew word that has many meanings, and some are now spiritual. But basically, the word means "to ride." That Hebrew word is Merkabah. The word Merkabah was popularized by how it was used in the ascension story of the prophet Elijah in Jewish history. It is also a word that has come to mean "Spiritual field of the Human Being" or "Vehicle that carries the Human Being." What is it, and what does it do?

The Human Field

The Merkabah is huge. It is eight meters wide (26 feet), and every Human Being has one. Here's what it is: The Merkabah is the multidimensional field which surrounds the Human Being. It is created by hundreds of trillions of identical DNA molecules, which also have tiny fields of their own. The DNA molecules are identical, all through the body, and they combine to create a much larger field around the body. The field is a multidimensional field that reflects the DNA's record of your body's many facets. Within its field is the patterning of the health of your body, your Akashic energy, your chemical inheritance, and of course, your spiritual attributes and soul energy. It's almost a full blueprint of YOU now, and in the past. It is this Merkabah that is your Innate. Your esoteric DNA collectively, is Innate.

The Whole Package

DNA cannot be seen as molecule by molecule. It's not separated from the whole. Think of it: Every molecule of DNA is unique and identical, so it's YOU. It's a collective essence of YOU. Let me tell you something: DNA (Innate) "knows" when there is a predisposition of when you are going to die. This is not a programmed certainty, but a potential product of your life lesson (and can always be changed). It's the field (Merkabah) around you who will "give up the ghost," not the brain. Sure, if the heart stops, nothing continues and there is death. If you have great body trauma, there is death. However, in other cases, the point at which someone dies is extremely complex. Sometimes it makes no sense at all when death occurs, and those who have seen it over and over in hospitals know that there is something else going on within the body.

Have you ever known a person to die because of grief? What bodily function caused that? If you say the heart, you would be right, but it's the emotional heart – which is involved in the Triad, not the biological heart. I'm going to introduce something I will call death intelligence. When Innate sees suffering ahead without hope, rather than go through more suffering, there's a shutdown command. That's Innate. That's the Smart Body, and indeed, it's really smart.

Listen: The same Innate is coming back in the next lifetime, because it's connected to the soul, and the pineal, and all that is. Your Merkabah has attributes of your life in the past, just like your soul does. It is the same one as the last time. You carry around a differently patterned Merkabah each time you are on the planet, but you have the same one as you did in the last life. Now, go figure that out! As I mentioned to you, this is difficult, because this is the mechanics of a multidimensional reality. Spiritual things are ALL multidimensional, and it's so beautiful to know that the you, the core of you, and who you are, gets passed to your next body over and over. Now you know how you can sense that you are an Old Soul. Your Innate knows.

If you could really meet you in a past life, and many of you have, you meet each other. You have different faces, but the same Merkabah, same soul, same Innate. Innate knows everything about every single lifetime you've had. Innate knows you better than you know your own self, and when you start getting in touch with

Innate, this is when things start to happen for you. This includes the ability to activate the Youth Template. Are you listening? It's going to happen.

Longer Life Is Ahead

Humanity is going to start living longer for a number of reasons. There will come a day when quantum energy can be used for amazing life extension and healing. This will be artificial activation with other fields that are quantum, and partial rejuvenation will be the result. This will echo that which was done in Lemuria at the Temple of Rejuvenation. We told you it was coming back! Some will say, "*Kryon, I thought we would be able to do this for ourselves? Why should we have any kind of outside rejuvenation machines?*" Dear ones, it's the same reason that you needed them in Lemuria. There were no "Old Souls" back then, and it was like training the DNA of those who were first timers, so they could rejuvenate and last longer. In the future, you won't just have Old Souls on the planet. Hardly! Those who are just arriving, and many who have only had a few lifetimes won't have the spiritual or Earth experience to work this puzzle for themselves. There will be those who can, and those who can't, activate the Youth Template. This should make sense to you. Not everything is generic, and the "same pill for everyone" strategy you have in chemistry-based medicine won't work. This is the linear approach that gets you into so much spiritual and moral trouble on the planet now. "One way for everyone." How has it worked for you so far?

For the Old Souls reading, this is your legacy: To become Human Beings who have DNA working in a far higher efficiency than now, and to be able to activate your own template, and live very long lives. How many times have we told you this? The consciousness of the Human Being, when fine-tuned, will take on the attributes of what you have called "the Masters of the planet." You will live a very long time. Now you know why the Masters and prophets lived so long. They had a Merkabah – an Innate – working at a very high percentage. And ... they were humans, just like you. Connect the dots. This is your future.

Stem Cells – Secrets Are Hiding

"*So, Kryon, where do stem cells fit into all of this?*" [Kryon laugh] Dear ones, that's where the templates are! That's where the templates are! What you call stem cells are in every single cell you have. You searched for this in a very linear, but logical way: You tried to gather them from embryos, since this is the start of life. Then you found they were in the umbilical cord – same logic. Now some scientists are saying they are everywhere! Basic stem cells are the blueprint for the body, and the Youth Template is within them.

Working with stem cells is the future, for that's where the template is. It is being investigated all over the planet, but many are still turning to outside cell sources. Instead, there will come a time when you use only your own stem cells, instead of from any other source, because it is your own cells that have the template that you really want. It's the ONLY template that will bring full rejuvenation. When you call someone else's phone number, you may get results and information. But when you call your own number, you get ... YOU.

Remember the information given above? Quantum sources are what activate quantum cellular processes. This is the key to the activation of the template. Your consciousness is quantum, and so are some things that researchers are discovering.

What Is Coming

There are things coming you don't expect. "*When are they coming, Kryon?*" The answer is, yes. The actual answer is, "When you allow them to come." When there's enough light on the planet, when these discoveries will not be weaponized, that's when you'll get them. "*When will that be, Kryon?*" When you create it, dear ones.

Right now you are in a profound transitional energy and you are in a struggle with basic light and dark. You know this. Some say, *"Kryon, you paint a much too simple picture of what is happening."* Not really. Currently, it's really basic: Will you choose slavery, horror, control, war, drama and death as your living scenario, or will you choose a consciousness of benevolent compassion and caring for each other? Will you allow others to select what you believe, and hold death over your families as punishment for noncompliance, or will you choose a higher road? Will your society learn a more elegant compassionate way to work with the puzzle of how to protect yourselves from lower consciousness action [crime], or not? Look at your news. You call that elegant? It's simply basic light and dark.

There are inventions coming that will forever make police work more workable for both sides. There will be far more humane ways of controlling those out of control, which will never result in death or bodily damage. There will be systems of vetting those who have authority, so it will be known how they "think" about others. All this seems to be science fiction now. But you will see what I'm speaking about. What do you think will happen when the Merkabah can be seen and analyzed? This is a hint.

When this transition time is over, and light is more predominant on this planet, that is to say, when integrity starts to win over non-integrity, things will begin to shift dramatically and very fast. You will see it in business, in government, and in how people treat each other. You'll start to see shifts of what people will accept and what they won't. It's the people who will then start to change the systems that have been unchanged for hundreds of years.

These things are in the works now. Some of what we speak of has actually been discovered now. I can tell you this, because Kryon does not reveal things that are not yet discovered. They have to have been discovered or thought of by humanity first, and typically, they're at their infancy and it will take a long time before they are refined. You should know that the template has been seen.

Unexpected Evolution

"Kryon, what will the template do biologically?"

The answer is, "exactly what you think it will do." Eventually, cell rejuvenation will be almost perfect throughout the body. This is the design of the template. The telomeres will not shorten, and the body will not age. Death will occur because it's time, and not because systems stop functioning. *"Kryon, this is going to create social problems! This won't work. Population explosion is exponential! Too many people right now, and not enough food. That's crazy talk about living hundreds of years."*

May I say this one more time? "Oh how 3D of you!" Listen, eventually you'll figure out what creates babies, and you'll be wiser for it. Other planets have done it, and even your own Ancients did it! A wiser Akash creates a wiser procreation scenario. Look for close to zero population growth even now in some of your first-world societies. Population growth numbers are only exponential, because you have made it so with low consciousness. It's not some mathematical formulation over which you have no control.

Discoveries are also at hand regarding how to create food for the planet in multidimensional ways. Food has DNA, too – connect the dots. Do you know what happens when you expose seeds to multidimensional energies that are benevolent? It's not a GMO. The plant itself accepts it as a benevolent sign, just like Innate with its template. Do you think that the life force of plants might also have something like you have? Can you imagine growing perfect crops, five, six times the yield, with no pesticides at all? What a concept! Is it possible that Human consciousness can be even extended to affect plants and animals? Experiments already show it can be done. This is just the beginning.

I have given you a glimpse into a beautiful future. Many who hear or read this say, "*I wish it were true. But Humans have always messed it up.*" Dear ones, if you have an attitude such that you don't expect much from others, then others won't give you much. This is how all consciousness on the planet works, but especially now. Your expectations are the rudder on your boat of life. If you expect storms, then they will come, as ordered. If you expect benevolence, even though there is not yet an indication of solution, you are actually creating the solution by your expectations. This is metaphysics, and it's what many of you have been teaching for years. So now is the time to practice it!

Those in front of me who are listening to this now, are Old Souls. They are all saying the same thing: "*Oh Kryon, it can't come too soon. Please, let's have it now. Kryon, when, when, when?*" I want you to be quiet for a moment. Relax. All of you will be there. All of you! Remember, this is your future. When you experience it, you may look a little different, but you're going to be there. [Laughter]. You are not going to miss this!

Dear ones, you are an Old Soul, if you are reading this. You are not finished with this planet. You're going to be in this future, do you hear me? I want you to get ready for it; I want you to celebrate it; it's going to happen. I want you to see the truth in this channelling. I want your Innate right now to check me out. Your Innate is a powerful discernment engine, and it will let you know if these things are true. When you get the chills that say "yes," then join me in celebration of what is to come.

And so it is.

"Blessed is the Human Being who feels they are part of this compassionate change on the planet. For they are in control of the future, and that is why there are congratulations all around, and a party in this room."

Kryon

Chapter Six

Conceptual DNA

A huge part of the evolutionary potential of our future is moving from a linear consciousness to one that thinks more conceptually. Many have said that we have a DNA that is moving out of 3D into a multidimensional potential. What does that mean? Kryon again discusses how our DNA has not evolved into its full potential. In fact, it's only "working" at a one-third efficiency. That starts to explain why we continually war, but never learn from it. It also explains why we have not "discovered" the elegance of what our DNA really can do for us, as Human Beings. Our DNA is "who we are, and unique to each of us." Kryon tells us that we now have the potential of having our DNA begin to evolve, to reflect the original blueprint. The results? Read on...

Lee Carroll

Chapter Six

"Conceptual DNA"

Kryon Live Channelling
Given in Portland, Oregon

July 20, 2013

Greetings, dear ones, I am Kryon of Magnetic Service. There is a larger audience here than you know. One of the attributes that we have described before is that we present ourselves to those in a group who have given pure intent to listen. You [this group] will create another energy. In this particular case, we call it the *Kryon entourage*. We don't identify this very often, but in this particular case, it's filled with those you know. Tonight will be a congratulatory message, filled with information about that which is cellular and chemical, but a message that could not have been given before this year. So the ones in the entourage who come into this room at this moment will mainly be esoteric – all of those who participated in life with you – ones who you've loved and lost. These include the parents and the parents before them. We say this, because they are also Lightworkers of their own on the other side of the veil, and they knew about the potential you would be here at this time of the Great Shift.

This entire concept is confusing to the Human Being's linear thinking. Some of you have said, *"Well, in the cycle of life, the ones you speak of have probably incarnated yet again, and they are on the planet with other lifetimes now."* In a linear fashion you would be correct, but dear ones, a piece of their soul never leaves the other side of the veil, and that is the part that is here today. So we invite them into this place at the moment, and many you will feel them, as they press upon you with their hands and their love and ask you to listen, listen, listen. Today is a message, a profound message, about the evolution of the Human Being.

We've given you information in the past that we now wish to clarify and enhance so you will have positive things to look forward to in the future. However, before we even begin with a new premise, we will review with you what we have described over and over about what is happening to the Human Being. We need you to know that there is precedent here, in that we have seen this before. So we know the potentials of what we speak, and the reality of it all. At the same time, we can tell you that we have no idea when you're going to allow these things to fully be developed.

 Humanity is going through massive consciousness shift [past 2012], and the time it takes to work through it totally depends upon free choice. This particular transition will last as long as you make it [last]. It always depends upon how hard the dark part of the duality decides to fight against you. The old energy of the planet will fight these changes, and it will fight them, perhaps, even to the death. That is to say, that a generation may have to be gone completely before some of these things will happen.

Old traditions and ways take a long time to disappear, and sometimes it requires even what you saw in history with the Israelites in the desert – when they had a forty-year period of time where one generation had to completely leave before another could be taken to the promised land. The reason? *You could never take the consciousness of slaves into the promised land.* A new generation that had never been slaves in Egypt had to be born and raised in a new energy – fed every day – taken care of and loved. This was in order for them to move into the lands where they would settle. That is not just a metaphor, but a good example of what you face now. How long will it take? This will not be what we address today.

Changing DNA

Today we address what is going to happen, and what has happened before to those who have gone through what you are facing. We set the full premise and describe what we have said before: Your DNA, right now as a Human Being, is operating at approximately thirty to thirty-one percent of its full capacity or efficiency. One hundred percent would be the "perfect Human," so that is as high as it goes. That would represent the DNA of the Masters who walked this planet, who could manipulate life, death, and physics. We told you that this current low efficiency was because of the free choice that you have always had to create the consciousness of your planet and society. The consciousness of humanity is tied directly to that which exists physically on the planet, including the percentage of your DNA which you enjoy. Therefore, what you think, you create. Through eons of time, humanity has settled to thirty percent or so.

Now, here's what I want to tell you that may be interesting: A discovery was made last September (2012). Science now finally understands what we told you years ago: Ninety percent of your DNA is *information,* not chemical codes. Ninety percent of your DNA is like the instruction manual – the control panel which modifies the protein encoding parts, that make all your genes. So you now have the validity, by science, that ninety percent or more of your DNA are the instruction-sets for the rest, and that is what we told you initially back in 2010.

Now, here's what I want you to be very, very clear about: Because you are operating at only thirty percent, most would think in a linear fashion and say, *"That means we're going to start improving, and science is going to look at it chemically and see this."* So I'm going to give you this information: No you're not. Let me explain why.

The information that you carry around in your DNA right now is one hundred percent of the whole. The manual for the perfect Human is complete and stored in your DNA, but the consciousness of humanity is only allowing thirty percent of it to be used. So, although you carry one hundred percent around with you, only thirty percept of it is "engaged" in your reality. As the DNA begins to change over time, through some of these new attributes I'm going to talk about yet tonight, it then captures or starts to use more of the instructions that are *already there*.

Proof of this whole notion of "complete DNA" are the so-called miracles that are seen with Human Beings, called *spontaneous remission*. Suddenly, and without much understanding, a sick person will totally heal themselves, completely and overnight – or the disease will simply disappear. Dear ones, all they have done is, for a moment of time, capture and use one hundred percent of their own DNA! So, what many would attribute to "a miracle of God," is something the Human did. Every so often, a Human Being, through an anomaly of their own creation, will shift to one hundred percent for a moment, and then "a miracle" will occur. However, you are not understanding that the Human simply saw what was available, and did it. The so-called miracle is actually normal! Note that it is usually in an emergency situation, and note that consciousness did it, not chemistry.

I want you to cognize and understand some issues, as I tell you a little more about what is going to happen. We have given you information in the past about what to expect with some of your evolving DNA. But almost all of the information we have given you is about communication to your Akash [past-life record]. We have told you that your DNA is going to start reading the Akash differently, and that the *wall* that exists between death and birth is going to be lifted slightly. Then, when you come back into the planet, you will begin to remember what you learned the time before.

This will serve the Old Souls best, because they will awaken early in life, and not have to re-visit the lessons that they had from the last time around.

We've also told you that, as babies, you're going to start to walk sooner, *remember* to read, and even remember that a hot stove is something to stay away from. You will have an increase in instincts, like the animals do, and the Human baby will not be quite as helpless as it is now. We identified this as Akashic inheritance, or Akashic remembrance.

We extended it to food. We told you that some of you were being given information about *spiritual* diets. Your most profound past lives, where you lived a very long time in one place, has food that your Akash wants today! We told you that, quite often, the food of your land [where you live today] actually goes against what your Akash wants. Even when you try to eat the *healthy* food around you, it may not actually agree with you. Some of you will find foods that revert to a kind of food that you were never attracted to before! However now, in a new energy, the Akash is starting to show itself with odd food choices, and you're enjoying it! It might ask for no meat or some meat, or it may require a different way of thinking or cooking. Listen: It doesn't mean it's spiritual! There is no "Spiritual Diet." Sometimes, your past Akashic attributes want meat! It just means that it is an Akashic remembrance of past body health. Now, that's still about Akashic remembrance, isn't it? This is still a review.

Chemically

So now, let us move to what will happen chemically to your body, with an increased percentage of activity of the *intelligence* of your DNA in place. Indeed, Intelligence is the word, and I want to talk about the *body intelligence*, which we call *Innate*. You're going to start getting closer to this "intelligent body." The veil will start to lift between the consciousness body and the Innate. The things that you muscle-test to find out today, will be intuitive tomorrow. The veil between the corporeal body and the Innate body is going to start to become more transparent, and you're going to start knowing intuitively about what's going on inside you. This has to do with intelligent DNA. That is, DNA which starts to work conceptually, instead of reactively, and it becomes less linear and a little more quantum [multidimensional].

Food

Some of you are enjoying what we have called Akashic inheritance and food remembrance, but with reservations. This is because you're intolerant to the certain kinds of foods you are trying to go toward. Now, the intolerance is caused from DNA that is not conceptual. It simply creates a 3D body which is allergic because of traditions in your existing culture, and it keeps you eating what you are used to. It's really just reacting to food it doesn't recognize, and that is actually a survival instinct. This makes it a bit dysfunctional, and that is puzzling to most.

The principles of an Akashic inheritance wanting a different food, yet being allergic to it, don't really seem to mix. But if DNA is starting to become more intelligent, it will analyze what you are doing with your Akash and throw away those things which create intolerance. So, suddenly you may have chemistry that is smarter about what you are trying to do. What I am saying is that some of you are going to find in your journey of the next years, that the things you were told to stay away from, in an earlier part of your life, are suddenly okay to eat! This is an *intelligent* DNA. It *knows* that you may need these "past-life" foods to balance your body better. Life will be a lot easier for you, if you can eat these foods without being intolerant. This is "intelligent DNA," which is now conceptual about who you have been in the past.

So the Innate readjusts the very metabolic system of what your body is supposed to be allergic to. This improvement and elimination of past-life food allergy reactions is created due to DNA becoming smarter. The increase in efficiency picks up a couple of higher operating percentage points, and it's a smarter *conceptual DNA* that is more tuned to your consciousness. It's going to show itself to be this way not just here, but also in the next subject, which is the immune system.

The Immune System

Your immune system right now is fairly basic. It operates, but it's fairly ignorant. It puts out fires. It doesn't ask where they came from; it doesn't ask how smart they are; it just puts them out. That's a metaphor for what invades your body that would cause the white blood cells to race to the scene and battle the metaphoric fire of unbalance or disease. In many cases it wins, as designed, and helps save your life almost on a daily basis. For, your immune system is geared to fight that which it knows about, and the simplest of bacteria that you live with are held at bay because of your immune system.

Some of the *original* vaccinations that you have taken have actually helped this, and they have created a whole series of additional *soldiers* to fight the disease battle, but it's still a very linear process. The immune system recognizes there's a fire and it goes and puts it out. But dear ones, that's not good enough to put out the fire called *cancer*. Why? Because cancer is a conceptual invader. It's an invader with a plan, and it's smart.

Some viruses can take over the cells' functioning parts, and some will even trick the immune system. In the case of cancer, you have growth which cannot be controlled, which often disguises or fortifies itself – encasing itself so the larger white blood cells don't see it, or if they do, they can't even get in. It's like a fire within a bubble that is impenetrable and it burns out of control and grows and grows and grows. Sometimes, a conceptual virus (including cancer) will be "cured" in one place, only to regroup and move to another. It's smart, and has a plan.

If the immune system were conceptual, it would see the cancer for what it was – what it was doing – and put out the fire. If the immune system were smart enough to be conceptual, it would see the *plan* of the virus and would thwart it by being smarter.

Now, all this smartness currently resides in the instructions in every molecule of DNA in your body. There are trillions of them, and they are all unique to you. In order for this evolution to happen, DNA itself is going to have to become a little more multidimensional, and we're going to get to that. As long as it stays in the linear state it's in now, and within the 3D chemistry that you are used to, you're not going to see much of an improvement. But as it becomes a little more multidimensional and picks up more of the instructions that it can now *see*, it will be ready to "outsmart" any conceptual virus. That's a promise. Use your spiritual logic. Do you think the highest evolved creature on the planet is supposed to have a system that is so ignorant that simple viruses can wipe out civilizations? Does this sound correct to you? If you were the Creator, would you build in a weakness like this?

This evolvement represents the Human Being growing into an entirely different creature. It's one you wouldn't recognize perhaps, if you came back in a couple of hundred years, or perhaps if you had a time machine to go forward. You will see the differences. One is linear, one is not. Humans will be much healthier and live far longer in the future.

The Common Cold

"Oh, that's good news, Kryon. I love it! It means that we're finally going to cure the common cold." Well, unfortunately, you're not. This is not profound information, and you should know it by now. The cold is a recalibrating device to balance you. It's needed and it's necessary, and all of you will continue having colds. If you have too many, your body is telling you that it's a little out of balance

and keeps trying to recalibrate. But you can have a cold as little as once or twice a year, and that is a good balance.

Your common cold recalibrates your system – not just one system. It develops antibodies for certain kinds of things, antibodies that are then fresh and good to go to work, and you need it. It's an irritant, but it doesn't kill you and it doesn't have to develop into something bigger. However, it will always be there. It's part of a balanced system.

The Body Clock

The one that you're going to like the best is the recalibration of the body clock. You're working at thirty percent, and you live a certain amount of years. Do I have to paint a picture for you? You're designed to live a lot longer. Now, in three dimensions, smart biologists will go after what they believe is the cause of aging, and in 3D, they're right. For at an efficiency of thirty percent, DNA shortens the telomeres with every cell rejuvenation division. The chromosome itself starts to become morphed into something less than it was at birth. So, you no longer have a fresh, complete unit any more. Instead, it's getting old. It's a copy of a copy. You age. The biologists see this shortening as the issue; however, it's only the result of a greater issue. You are not working at full efficiency.

Now, what we have told you before in the past is that, in the instruction-sets of the DNA are the *stem blueprints* for every kind of cell in the body. We have used the term "blueprints" to represent the metaphor of the designer's plans. So these blueprints exist in you now, and they represent a fresh, new, perfect cell – one that was with you when you were born. However, these blueprints are not being used, and your system continues to make copies instead of originals.

However, as your body starts to increase in efficiency, there will be a newer kind of regeneration paradigm. The system will become more intelligent, and will slowly begin to use the original instructions for a new molecule, instead of making a copy. Your regeneration will be far better! The result of this is a slowing of the aging process. It's a slowing that you can see now, and those around you will mention it, and your neighbors and loved ones can see it, too. You are not getting older as fast as they are. How do you like it so far?

Now, this can only happen if that part of your DNA which used to be linear, becomes a little more multidimensional, and now we're going to talk about that.

Multidimensional DNA?

So it seems, does it not, that the basis to all this change is beginning to pull you out of the paradigm of a three-dimensional chemistry system? Your current system is only reactive. One chemical reacts to another and creates something else. This even includes synapse [thinking], and so you're also looking at what we would call "reaching the intellectual high-point of the brain." How *high* can you think? Is there a limit? We don't speak of linear things, but rather, conceptual things. Right now there is a limit.

The DNA molecule is not a quantum particle – hardly. It's also not going to become multidimensional and vanish into a worm hole. But the actual molecule of DNA has been shown to have subtle multidimensional properties. So greatly is this acknowledged, that there is an entire branch of biological scientists called "quantum biologists." So the idea of your DNA starting to have some additional abilities that might broach 3D and 4D, is not that new.

My partner has told you that ancient Tibetan numerology teaches, that humanity has only identified up to the number 33 in that system. That is a master number with a specific definition, but the next master number, 44, is a mystery and has no definition. In fact, no master number above 33 has a definition. If you look at the number of master numbers, 11 through 99 (nine of them), then you realize that a DNA working at 30% is the same kind of scenario as the master numbers that only go to 33. In other words, you're not even halfway there. So, as an example, the synapse of your brain, that part which is in 3D, seems to be working well. It's the multidimensional part that is needed to grasp the concepts of the numerology of 44 and 55 – it's all related. I'm here to tell you that past 2013, that's what's going to start happening with humanity – higher wisdom, and concepts that have never been *seen* before. The ceiling will be raised on how high a Human can think past linearity.

Now, how is this going to happen, and what is required? It's what you're already doing, Old Soul. You're sitting here listening to these kinds of messages because of this, and right now, these things seem academic. However, they are in the works. We can't tell you when these things are going to happen, but watch for them – here they are – they are coming. Perhaps you'll leave this place and you'll say, *"I love the information, but I'd sure like it to happen now."* Does it help if I told you that you'll all see it? When you see it, you may not look the way you look now [Kryon laugh], but you'll be here. You'll be here, because that's what Old Souls do. They keep coming back to participate in the victory!

The Time Capsules in DNA

I want to tell you about the time capsules in DNA. In the instruction-sets that are not visible to science, there lurks something called *time capsules* in your DNA. These are releases of what we will call "Enablements," and they are triggered by Human consciousness. They are *time capsules,* because they are being released at "the right time." Many would say, *"What? DNA is connected to Human consciousness?"* Yes, this is what we have been saying all along. Why do you wish to separate consciousness from your chemistry? You already know that you can change your health by positive thinking, so how do you think that works? Your chemistry is listening!

To make things even more confusing, this is all linked together to what is called the *Gaia consciousness,* which is the only measurement you have of planetary consciousness. All humanity must shift and change only a little bit in order to release the time capsules in your personal DNA. So it's hard for you to do this alone, if not impossible. This change takes its cue from the Crystalline Grid of the planet. This is the grid that remembers Human action and responds to Human emotion. So, Gaia is involved with all of these things. Do you now begin to realize why Gaia, or nature, was so important to the indigenous and the Ancients? However, remember that Gaia has already started to change. I am here to work with the grid – Gaia. It's to prepare you for a higher consciousness. Are you understanding the connection? So what's in the time capsules? It's the "rest of what you should have had" that was missing, due to a lower consciousness. You should know that full mastery is there in your DNA, just waiting to be released when you are ready.

Here we are again with a puzzle: What came first, Gaia energy or Human energy? As Humans change their personal consciousness and intent, as they become more compassionate, Gaia changes. It already has. Isn't it interesting what the Ancients had to say about the prophecy of *The Eagle and the Condor?* The prophesies were not about humanity, but rather, they were about the planet. Do you understand? It told of the wisdom from one place on the planet, moving to another. The prophesy says that the moving of the Kundalini of the planet would be needed, if humanity passed 2012. Some called it *"The Journey of the Feathered Serpent,"* or *"The Awakening of the Puma."* They were not talking about DNA, but instead, about Gaia, because that is the link to you. So the answer to the above puzzle question is, *both.* It's not a linear process. It's interactive, and one affects the other.

This change in Gaia is what is beginning, and it's already starting to enhance Human DNA. I came to alter the magnetic grid, when it appeared that you would indeed pass the marker of 2012.

The magnetic grid is part of Gaia. It affected the Crystalline Grid, and that is related to Human consciousness. Even your science of today is starting to see this link! The magnetic grid reacts to mass human consciousness.[1]

Look at your children, for they are different from past generations. Grandparents, are your grandchildren different than your children were? Absolutely! These new-generation children are beginning to have more conceptual thinking, and the very synapse of the brain is already starting to change. They are seeing better ways of doing things, and the actual creation of neural pathways is different today. Their DNA is working better than yours does or did, in conceptual ways. So your job is to continue the compassion that you are developing, which is curing the planet of its disease of war. This *Gaia Effect* is curing the planet of those things that do not sit well with integrity. It's Pachamama, Mother Earth, and the beginning of the procreation of wisdom on the planet. These changes are going to start to bring better understanding and the increase of wisdom, which will help to solve the puzzles of life. Gaia changes, the Crystalline Grid changes, you change, and that, then, is passed to your children in ways you haven't really thought of.

A New Kind of Inheritance

Here's some very good news you should know: The *system of life* is beginning to change even further. When time capsules are released in your DNA, some through new birth and some through the intent of the Old Souls, there is a higher wisdom factor in your consciousness. This has an effect on your DNA, which starts to work better. As indicated above, you won't age nearly as fast. You're going to see it in your own DNA, and many will know it's happening, through seeing their own peers go into old age far earlier than they do.

---

1   www.kryon.com/122-1

The time capsules that are released, the new enablements from that pool of information that used to be the "Junk DNA – 90 percent," will stay enabled and be inherited! Therefore, none of your offspring will have to re-learn the wisdom or compassion that you are learning now. As they use your DNA inheritance on the planet, it will be passed to their offspring, as well. A new kind of inheritance! You might even call it *quantum inheritance,* if you wish. This is truly the fast track to an enlightened society.

If there were no duality on the planet, you would have had a much higher-working DNA in as few as five generations. Today, you would work at fifty percent enablement, because an advanced instinct of the Human Being is to become more conceptual and use it for survival of higher thought. But duality slows this down, since you must make decisions that contain attributes of both light and dark. As long as the old duality is present, it tends to restrict all growth, which keeps the time capsules from opening. Therefore, old duality must change. In fact, it is changing greatly (as we have channelled before). What's interesting is that duality also responds to conscious intent, and so your battle against the dark will be totally the result of what you expect. It's getting very immediate, dear ones.

The time since 2012 has been tough for many of you. Old Soul, if you really knew why it has been so tough, and if you understood the full impact and the profundity of it all, you'd go home and have a party! There, you would congratulate yourselves for doing the unthinkable – creating the seeds of a planet that will ascend. You have been working this puzzle for a very long time.

Slowly, you have been creating, planting, and growing the seeds on your planet that will lead to an Earth civilization without war. Oh, you'll never get along completely, but your solutions will never again be to kill each other in war. That's a dysfunctional solution that has only brought about more war. This "no war" potential is the one we see, even today. If you look at your societies of only a few generations ago, the solution to world issues was to go to war first. Only the biggest and most powerful would win the prize. Now, it is becoming the last thing you would do, and there will come a day when it just won't happen at all. Can you imagine a reallocation of funding for society, when there are no more weapons of mass destructive war? This is in your future. Don't look at immediate current events to see this. Look at slow generational change.

Imagine a time capsule being released that changes "how high you can think!" Imagine that your DNA might do a better job at broadcasting a quantum field around its own cellular structure, and could make the immune system intelligent, bringing about a marriage between the conscious brain and the Innate. There is no name for this effect yet. Oh, but there will be! Scientists will observe the change, and they will label it. When this starts to occur, dear ones, you'll remember this channel. You might even laugh at the fact that my partner had no name for it yet, but you will have a name. This is because it's part of Human evolution, and sociologists will grab it and name it.

Do you understand why this is a celebration? Do you understand why the entourage in this room, which has been with you since the moment we began, is applauding? Do you understand that this particular message could never have been given to you in 2012? Not like this. Because now, I can tell you what's going to happen, but before then, it was only a potential. *"Kryon, you mean it's now more than a potential?"* Yes. Today it's far more than a potential, and the reason I can tell you that is because there are some Humans walking around right now who have a much higher percentage of DNA than thirty percent. I'll call them *quantum prodigies*. These are children who are going to live longer and not catch many diseases, and you'll study them and put them under microscopes, but you're not going to see anything different.

Someday, when you get the quantum invention that we told you about before, you're going to see the "field." Some of you have understood this message and some of you have not. For those who have not, I will say this: Be patient with the love of God, and understand that revelation is often a slow process. For those who have, I will summarize it and say, "Blessed is the Human Being who feels they are part of this compassionate change on the planet. For they are in control of the future, and that is why there are congratulations all around, and a party in this room."

Twenty-three years ago, when I first came to you, these things were only potentials, but today, they are a reality. I would not tell you of these things, if they were not accurate and true. I also understand, dear Human Being, that you're very impatient, and that you want it now. Soon, it will be "now" and you will be here to participate in all of it.

And so it is.

"What if your Akashic Remembrance started to know what's good for you, instead of simply blasting you with issues to correct, or things that you must "go through" that are ultra-dramatic? This is a new paradigm, involving a more elegant role for the Akash."

Kryon

Chapter Seven

Conceptual Consciousness

Seven days after the channelling on Conceptual DNA, Kryon gave three new ideas about how our consciousness is going to start changing, for the New Human. Again, the change is from linear to conceptual, and how it might affect our future thinking. This message is more difficult to understand, since it deals with things that we are not seeing yet. When there is no frame of reference in our current life, it's then harder to imagine things that have not yet been conceived. The channelling deals with Akashic awareness, and even future reasoning. This is truly futuristic, but filled with promise for us all.

Lee Carroll

Chapter Seven

"Conceptual Consciousness"

Kryon Live Channelling
Given in Kansas City, Missouri

July 27, 2013

Greetings, dear ones, I am Kryon of Magnetic Service. You might notice that my partner doesn't seem to *prepare* for channelling. In an older energy, it was necessary to prepare for what happens corporeally to the Human body during the trance. In the past, it often had to be preceded by purification, so you saw a lot of the use of balanced breathing and other techniques to clear and purify certain parts of the brain. It would give needed oxygen to tell the body what was coming, and to prepare for a multidimensional experience. You will see that my partner doesn't do this.

The Channelling Experience

There are many who have said, *"Well, the posturing of the Human Being in a certain attitude, and the development (raising) of certain frequencies using meditation and toning, are needed to channel. This is the logical way it should be done, and it has been done this way throughout history."* They are correct! But you don't see him doing that, either. This would lead some to say, *"He's not doing it right!"* Others will say, *"He's not doing it at all!"* (Therefore, he is not channelling.) They would then use this as evidence that the channelling isn't real. We say it again: What does your own discernment say about this, not what others say?

You're starting to see some big shifts in all esoteric and meta-physical processes, and my partner is very aware of them. Four years ago (2009), he made a large shift: I asked him if *he was ready for the next level in vibration*. He was surprised, since he felt that the channelling was going well. I told him that he was simply putting Kryon in a box and turning the key when he sat down. He was linearizing Spirit, as so many do on the planet. Instead of reporting to a building on a certain day, wearing nice clothes, and praying or kneeling, he was doing the same thing by making Kryon active only when he was *in the chair*. I was not there when he was going about his normal life. He had created "Kryon In A Box."

His first challenge to this was: *"What else is there?"* This is when I asked him if he felt that the Masters who walked the Earth had *God in a box*, or if they carried the elements of the Creative Source with them all the time. It didn't take long for him to say *"Yes"* to the meld, and now he fully understands. That step is what we are talking about today. It's a step that is available to all, and it's a beautiful gift in this new energy. It's for everyone! It's especially nice for healers and readers, and those who are working directly with others. It is a melding of YOU and your Higher-Self, so that corporeally, you don't have to "prepare" your body to do things that are already there and ready to go. That's what is new, and that's what we wish to discuss today. Is it possible that, as you evolve in this new energy, there are parts of you that literally "come alive" with the timing of all this? Parts, perhaps, that have been there all along, but that were veiled in an older energy? Dear ones, the Human is designed to communicate with the Creator! The Human Being is designed to discover GOD INSIDE!

The Meld

The meld starts to change the way you think, and how you act. It starts to change how you age, and so many other things that you have not thought about! This is your future. So, this particular channelling, for the group tonight, and for those who wish to listen right now [the Kryon web site audios], has, again, to do with the changes that are coming in the Human Being. It's an extension of the information about how Humans are changing and evolving.

Human nature has you in a very strong duality, and you are not even aware of it. You are also in a spiritual box. Pretend for a moment: You are on your way to a spiritual meeting. What's happening in your consciousness? Some people are critical and complaining right up the place where the meditation starts. Then they are humble and spiritual. Then at the break, the temperature is wrong, the coffee is no good, and they wish there was more of this or that. The attitude is of disappointment and complaint. Then they go back to the meeting and become spiritual again. Welcome to "hidden duality" that many are not even aware of. Do you see the odd unbalance of this?

There are even those here, listening and reading, who don't fully realize this concept. How many Masters walked around in a complaining attitude? The meld is what bridges the gap in duality, and creates a Human who sees a much different world. Patience is not something you work on, as much as it is self-evident, in a consciousness that is relaxed with the things of Earth.

Refining a Concept

Before we get into this more, I want to pause a moment. I want to refine a concept for you of what is taking place right now. Where is my partner? Is he in the chair or not? The answer is, absolutely, he is in the chair. Where is my partner's consciousness, as I channel through him? In an older energy, many would say, *"Well, he had to go into the closet to get away from everything, because there is now a take-over of the body."* However, that's not true. Do you wish to know where he is? He is right in front of you. I am using everything he has to deliver this message. Corporeally, everything he has is filled right now with me, and that's the difference, dear ones. You don't *throw a switch* anymore and become someone else, and then have messages from beyond that are not part of your consciousness. He is still here, enjoying the meld. He is also somewhere else, as he has described before. But WE are working together.

So the meld took place and the difference in him has been noted by some, for as he walks around, he thinks differently; he sees people differently, and he knows it. He didn't expect it. It has given him a different perception about what things might be, in areas of which he has no knowledge. This is what we want to talk about, and it's difficult, because it does have minutia that is academic and hard to understand. Sometimes, it does not necessarily translate well into your linear language, but we use my partner's intellect and his ability to conceive what I'm giving you, and his ability to translate it accurately without filters, the best he can.

A Short Review

Old Souls are the ones who are most prone to listen to this information. Old Souls are the ones who are most prone to be in the chairs in front of me, and it doesn't matter how old they are physically. Some of the oldest souls on the planet alive today are under twenty. They have to be, dear ones, they have to be. Gone is the tradition that the elder in your group holds the best information. It simply is not the way it is, anymore. Respect your elders for their Earth knowledge and experience; but the Akashic elders in the group are the ones who have been here the longest, measured in lifetimes on the planet. They will have the wisdom of the ages, and will represent the Ancients like no one else can. That's part of what we want to talk about.

So, let us begin a short summary of what we were talking about last time in channel, when the subject came up about the spiritual evolvement of humanity. In order to cover this properly, we review:

Human DNA is only operating at a percentage of efficiency slightly over thirty percent. So, everything that is inside you that makes you YOU, is operating at less than half of what it was designed to do.

This condition is something you developed over eons of free choice, with a duality you created. You developed the balance of dark and light in your own consciousness (called duality). You have selected how well you think, and how much your societies are going to absorb the idea that compassionate thought can heal the planet. You select whether you are high-minded or medium-minded or low-minded. This is the attribute of free choice of the planet. This is the test and always has been. It a test of energy, and balance of dark/light consciousness. It's the test that is primary and basic, and is the one that is now shifting on the planet.

Dear ones, you're advancing so profoundly, as we have told you in the past, and evolving so quickly, that you are beginning to see the growth of Human intelligence and compassion in your societies right now. You're also going to see it at the corporeal level as well, because when Human DNA begins to work at a better efficiency, it's going to be obvious. We've given you other channels you can also study as a reference. The last one was titled "Conceptual DNA." In that one, we spoke of a corporeal Human Being who went beyond what we would call *linear immune reaction*. Linear immune reaction is where the white cells of the body see a problem, race to that problem, and fight it. That's pretty basic, but it's also as *smart* as that particular chemical process gets. The issue is that it may not be enough to solve the problem, because it is beyond the ability of the white cells to *perceive the concept of the invader.*

Viruses notoriously seem to be intelligent, for they seem to have *a plan.* However, the white blood cells only know how to sense, fight, and defend. They don't see any bigger picture. The cells don't know anything about cancers – how they operate, or that they may be immune to most defense cells! So, Conceptual DNA, then, becomes "smarter DNA," involving corporeal systems that *know* concepts. It creates a Human Being who can fight any virus and any disease, because it will have an immune system that is as smart as anything that can invade. It's conceptual. This is an evolvement of Human DNA, past thirty percent, moving more toward thirty-five and forty.

The Example

How many Masters do you know on the planet who died of a virus? Most of them died at the hands of other Human Beings. The Masters of the planet had DNA that operated far better than yours. Some had the ability to create or alter physical things around them, practicing the process of creating or altering matter though consciousness alone. The Human Being's mind can manipulate physics, and that was always the design. Consciousness is now understood to be able to alter the way light behaves, and mass consciousness [planetary] can actually alter the strength of the magnetic grid! [Global Consciousness Initiative] So, it's a "given" in certain scientific circles that consciousness is a "player" on the field of energy.

What do you think about spontaneous remission? What is it? How does it work? Does it require outside influence, or is it created internally? The answer is this: In spontaneous remission, you are seeing the DNA of a Human working close to one hundred percent, just for a moment. When it happens, it is unexplainable and miraculous to you, but you can clearly see the results, recognize it, and even document it. The Human can *clean themselves* of almost any disease, almost overnight! That was the review.

The Potentials of What Is Next

I want my partner to go slow here, for just recently, there have been channels in which I've given him information, but there were simply no words to explain it. When there is no definition or nomenclature for what he discusses, he must *dance* around it, in order to try to translate new concepts. Perhaps, he even makes up words or phrases to get across what we want you to know. Dear ones, we are giving you this channel in honor of the potentials to come. We want you to know that you've done something special on this planet. We want you to recognize that, over a period of time, humanity has always had the potential of shifting into far greater kinds of Human Beings than you've ever seen. This concept runs contrary to everything you've ever been taught. It runs contrary to some of your belief systems, that tell you you were born unworthy, and that God has judged you as such. It runs contrary to what people have said of the future of the planet. Ingrained in you is the idea that you're not going to make it. You're going to have to get over that, and this is part of the New Human.

I've got three concepts for you, which really continue the main concept of the evolution of Human DNA. However, instead of being called "Conceptual DNA II," this particular channel will be titled, "*Conceptual Consciousness.*" You have to understand that your DNA is responsible for the very synapse of your thought processes, and the instructions of how your brain works. The blueprint of how you cognize things, and how you work with each other, is in the DNA. Your DNA doesn't think for you, but rather, it establishes the construct of how everything works together. Can you conceive that the actual blueprint is changing? If so, can it now include more esoteric and multidimensional instructions? Let us discuss some esoteric things that are already present in your body, in order to give you the concept, that much of it is already in place.

We have mentioned in the past, that part of your body is called "Innate." You have called it the "Smart body," and it's the part that you muscle-test for information [kinesiology]. The Innate is beginning to meld with common consciousness at a three-dimensional level. All this means is, that eventually, you will have a far better idea of what is going on at the cellular level of your body, than ever before. This is coming. Doesn't it make sense, that this would be one of the evolved steps? There is a profound relationship, however, that is very esoteric, which is not necessarily on your mind at the moment. It is all about the Akash.

Akashic Conceptual Remembrance

The first evolvement attribute we wish to speak of is what we are going to call *Akashic Conceptual Remembrance*. Let's look at the Akashic Record within your DNA, and how it functions.

How many of you are aware of your past lives? The answer will be, "not many." You are here in an attitude of belief, knowing you are an Old Soul, but you can't necessarily identify your past lives, or pull out the ones that are most important or dramatic. At the moment, the Akashic Remembrance in your cellular structure is not all that smart. All it gives you is that which emotionally *sticks out*, due to it being dramatic. For Lightworkers, it often delivers a feeling of a *lack of self-worth*, because of these things that stick out. Old Souls, these are most often the feelings of your many battles with the old energy that you didn't win. So you sit here in an audience [those reading and listening] where most of you have something in common [lack of self-worth], which is something we have discussed before.

However, why is it that, seemingly, only dramatic issues of the past come to the surface of today's reality? The reason? It's because there is a linear remembrance in your Akash, which only allows for the negative things to stick out. What about the good parts? What about the many celebrations and joyful things in the past? They get beat back by the dramatic parts. The reasons is that the dark/light balance of the past was heavier than today.

You have a tendency to remember and dream about your past lives, where the issues of the past create some blockages today. Many times your past experiences were so profound in a past life, that there is still a residual of that same experience with you today. These issues become part of the healing that a past-life reader will help you with.

Now, consider for a moment, that all this is the way it works with DNA performing at only thirty percent or so [speaking of how DNA is not operating at full potential]. What if the Akashic and the Innate begin to work together, to create something that is more conceptual? An evolvement in DNA will begin to do just that. What if your Akashic Remembrance started to know what's good for you, instead of simply blasting you with issues to correct, or things that you must "go through" that are ultra-dramatic?

This is a new paradigm, involving a more elegant role for the Akash. Instead of delivering older dramatic energy, the Akash starts seeing the Human Being as an evolving spiritual part of the entire planet, and begins to deliver the things that you should *remember*, that are going to help you push the envelope of evolution and belief.

An Example: Let's say that you come into the planet in your next incarnation, and as you grow up, you start to remember the *concepts* of your past issues, and not the emotions of them. Instead of remembering snapshots of problems, it [the Akash] delivers to you the solutions you learned from having the problems. Do you understand what I'm saying? An Akashic Remembrance that is conceptual, working with Innate, will deliver to you the wisdom that you have as an Old Soul today, from the experiences you have had [in past lives]. For instance, let's say you severely burn your hand on a stove when you are a child. For your entire life, you won't touch a stove. When you reincarnate, instead of the Akash bringing you the drama of a burn, with all the pain, confusion and frustration, it remembers, *"Don't touch a hot stove."* In other words, it remembers *concepts of wisdom* from the past, instead of the *elements of drama that were involved in the lessons.* Some of you will have this by the time you are eight. For some, it will take a little longer. That's just one thing that's in store for the Old Soul the next time around. It's a potential for a real change in the way the Human body thinks and works.

"Kryon, is this new?" Not really. It's new to you in this age, but this is the way your DNA was designed and supposed to work, had you allowed it. Do you understand that, by passing the marker of 2012 into this new recalibrating energy, you have given permission to start a climb of efficiency in your DNA? It's important that you understand the changing potential of this planet at this time!

Be aware that this may take generations, dear ones, for your DNA to slowly change in this way. I'm giving you information that is going to happen on a timeline that you'll create through free choice and allowance. How hard is the old energy going to push back? As hard as you allow it to, within your changing energy. Yes, it will often slow you down, and we told you that. But spiritual evolution cannot be stopped and you're going to start to see it slowly happening. I'm not done. That's number one. Number two is the hardest one.

Future Potential Reasoning

Now, my partner, I just want you to go slow. [Kryon admonishing Lee to slow down.] I'm about to give you a concept that you've never experienced or thought about before, and it's the way synapses works in your brain. I'm even going to try to give you a name for it. *Future Potential Reasoning.*

The way Human Beings think, at the moment, is linear. Now, the brain is a beautiful computer and it's the fastest one on the planet. You're not aware of what it goes through to do what it does, but let me just briefly tell you about it: The Human brain is based upon experiences. It's a storehouse of everything you've ever done, to enable you to survive. It's simple, in some ways, and complex, in others. When a Human approaches a flight of stairs, the brain sorts through everything it has ever seen in order to recognize the stairs. When it recalls "stairs," it knows how to climb them, based on past experience, and all is well. If it had never seen stairs, your reaction would be entirely different.

You can imagine, as a baby develops and grows up, how many experiences the brain would have to have in order to remember and navigate normal things. All of this is linear. No matter what you do you in life, you are presented with all of the images and memories of your past, and the brain sorts through them at lightning speed to give you options. Then it calculates for you what to do next. You come into a room like this, and you see other people, chairs and other furniture you recognize. It's not a mystery. Your brain puts it in a perspective you have experienced before, so you can sit down, and you know how to do it. It's automatic.

Do you have any idea the amount of computation power it takes to do that? Imagine sorting through your entire life experience, so you can sit in a chair! That's what the brain does for you, and it's good at it. It's survival; it's protection. It helps you when you meet people, to say the right things that create friends and not enemies. Your brain sorts through reactions that you've had in the past, to conversations you have had, and the correct words you spoke that made a difference in the past. This is the linear brain at its best, and it suits you very well.

Now I'm going to present something new. Let's talk about chess. The chess master sits at the board. Now, this is a metaphor. The board represents the puzzles and realities of life which we're going to call 3D [even though it's 4D]. You live and you walk in

4D and the puzzles are based upon height, depth, width and time. All of these things are your reality, and this is how you think and work and play. You fit all of this into "the chess board of life," and your brain helps you to calculate what to do next, and you do it. It is all based on momentary survival. But now enters the chess master. A chess master evaluates the *potential reaction* of many moves [actions], and works a huge puzzle of "what if's." There may be five or six moves to intuit and project, depending upon the puzzle, before action is taken. How many people are involved in the puzzle, and what are the potential results?

Next, let's change the game: Instead of winning a chess game by capturing the other's players, the chess master will, instead, look at the highest potential of *solution of benevolence* of the situation. That will be the move that is selected. In other words, the winning move is now the move that will create solution of situation, instead of capturing a player's assets.

So, the first idea is, to measure or intuit immediate potential reaction to each of many moves. Now he looks at what might happen after he moves this way or that, and then does it again. He measures the potential future of what might happen, based upon his projections and experience and intuition. He's calling upon an innate ability that not many have. He has a mind that computes future potentials.

Now he's on his third move projection after the first potential moves. What will happen if this took place, or that took place, or he moved here or there? It requires a myriad of possibilities and potential reactions. But, instead of rules of the game, he must use intuition of what the players around him would do. Based on that, what is the highest potential of a solution around the move? What will others do?

Do you see where this is going? You're not a chess master unless you've got [at least] five moves ahead. The chess master of today has a certain amount of time to compute all this, and as he sits there, you can watch his brain working, as he looks around the board and examines his next moves [potential results]. However, in this new scenario, the new chess master (you) must look at every potential that might occur and what might happen – happen very quickly – and automatically make good, compassionate decisions, using a higher performing DNA. Can you imagine the brain power it will take for this?

Let's make this practical: Many of you have children, so let's use a common situation as a metaphor: Two young siblings, approximately a year to a year-and-a-half apart, are eating together. The dynamics are often the same anywhere on Earth, and the gender doesn't really matter at a certain age. They are natural adversaries. They are sitting at the table, and one does something the other really doesn't like. One hoards food, and won't give the cookie to the other. Parents, you have seen this many times. So the other, who is now irritated, yells, complains, and will grab at or take away the hoarded cookie. The first one will grab it back. Then the first one will swat the other and the other will swat him back. Soon, there's a contest going on, and discomfort, injury, crying, drama – and the mother must step in [and intervene]. I think you're familiar with the scenario and it's endless. It goes on all the time until maturity comes in through age or experience.

Now, I want to run the process again, and I want you to pretend that these children have evolved in a way that I have just described is possible. Think how this might be: The one child does something that the other child does not like. This is the same scenario, but right away, instead of grabbing the cookie, the hungry child has *intuitive Future Potential Reasoning*. With lightening speed, he runs the scenario of what happens if he grabs the cookie. He may not have the experience or the maturity, but he'll have potential reasoning and he will see that it will end badly, and he *won't* get the cookie. Not only that, he might have to go to his room because of an angry mother. He might even lose all cookie privileges! He got all the moves in a flash of understanding – so he does nothing – or he may simply leave the table. The cookie? He still wants it, and may find a way of getting it, but not by grabbing it from his sibling. The cookie will be eaten another time, perhaps by method of "reward" when there is no drama or competition [Kryon smile]. Smart kid! He also has the concept that there is more than one cookie, somewhere.

Why do I give you this? Why am I concentrating on this? Because, Human Being, this is a shift of basic Human nature! If you get to that point, do you understand why you're not going to war anymore? You won't, because you will know the future projection of death, destruction, sorrow and a bad outcome. So bad, you may even repeat it, to try to get back at the one who *started* it. A Human race, whose propensity and wisdom to walk away from the [action that] sparks conflict, will be a new Human race! I'm telling you that this is not that far away. Have you seen the hold-outs that you have right now in the world in the various countries that still want to make trouble? They represent a very old energy of the past. The planet looks at them and thinks, *"Why don't you join the Earth? That's not what we do anymore."* It's already occurring. That's a hard one.

Relationships

What about relationships? You won't have to guess as much, anymore! It will be instinctive and intuitive. Future Potential Reasoning will be lightning fast, and you won't even know you have it, except that you will think differently. When you meet someone for the first time, there's a protocol that Humans have. There's a small wall between the two of you that you have to work on, and test and try. All this, to see if another person could possibly [become] your partner. What if, instead, you were able to look inside and see the

God in them first? What if you could recognize past relationships! That's intuitive Akashic Remembrance at its best! It's coming. The very way you greet each other, what you can see within each another, and the ability to love one another, will almost be an open book to both of you. It's all going to eventually change, but I can't tell you when. I can't even tell you if you are going to be here in your current corporeal body. That's up to you, or how fast you change things. But I can tell you, that this is what's happening.

Subconscious Awareness

Here is a final concept: *Control Over Subconscious*. Right now, you don't have it. What some have called the not-self, and others have called the subconscious, is what we speak about. It's the part of you which is not you totally, but which lies under your thought. It's important, since it's often an irritant in your personality, because it gives you fear and mistrust, and affects how you live. It's often the "what if" part of your brain. "What if" you don't present a good face? "What if" you catch a disease? What if, what if, what if – so you stay at home and you do nothing. With help, you eventually realize that it isn't even *you* talking. The subconscious represents a very active duality. In the future, the conceptual Human is going to see all this for what it is, and put it into the back seat, where it belongs. That's a metaphor.

As you grow up and move forward in life, you won't have disturbing fears. For some of you, the agonizing doubts that you've tried to conquer all your life will be seen for what they are, and will be dropped. I know who's here and who is reading! Wouldn't it be nice to just identify it all and put it away? This will represent profound self-balance. These things I've just given you are starting to occur in humanity, and you're going to see some [people] with it, like many of the other changes I have spoken of.

Over a decade ago, my partner started talking about the new consciousness of children on the planet [Indigo Children]. At that time, there were already a lot of them. Now, most of them are that way. This is the way Human consciousness will evolve – generationally. Already on the planet, you're going to see these things, but within ten to fifteen years, the potential is, that it's going to be a lot more obvious than it is now. What it means, dear Human Beings, is that Human Nature is, indeed, changing. You'll call it many things. Psychologists will call it increased maturity. Indeed, that is the way it will look.

Scientists will also take a look at how you fight disease. The Human Being is developing immunity that is new, and part of a better performing DNA, but the scientists will never go to where I went today. A DNA that is starting to see the instructions clearer will work better. Oh, there's more, but not today.

The Old Soul

If things only changed in the ways I told you today, it would be enough to create a life that would be amazingly different than anything you're used to now. But there is much more. The final thing I will say to you is that you don't have to have another body in another life, to make this happen. If you believe in spontaneous remission, you know that anything we're talking about right now is available to you in real time, Old Soul.

We don't want you to have to leave this life and come back, in order to facilitate these things. We want you to create them now. See these things as possible in your bodies, dear ones, and claim them! There are those in this room who have healed themselves from disease, so why do you stop there? Take a look at what the potentials are. It will change your countenance, your fears, how people see you, how you react (or don't) and help you become a model of the future Human. That's what Old Souls are here for. That's my message of the day.

There is such an honoring of your process! Do you know how I can tell you these things? I've seen it before! You're not the first planet to have graduated into this situation. Did you know that life in the galaxy is based on DNA? You're going to see this, and laugh at your presumptions. It's everywhere, and you're going to see that as well. As soon as you find any other life that's microbial anywhere on any moon or planet in the future, and analyze it – you're going to find the double helix. Get ready for it. We've seen this before, so we know the potentials before you.

And so it is.

"If you're an old soul, you can feel it. If you can feel it, you're an old soul. Congratulations to all of you for being who you are. You are the ones who will change the planet."

"The Old Soul Defined" Bali, Indonesia – March 29, 2015

Source: www.kryon.com/old-soul-defined

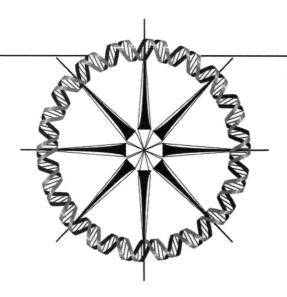

*"Human Beings are going to start having
the same kind of attributes of consciousness
that your cells enjoy. They'll be connected.
They will start to know what the other one
is thinking. Not personally or privately, but
intellectually and cooperatively. Common
sense will be the guide."*

Kryon

Chapter Eight

The Energy of the Future

Kryon continues to give us more and more information about what is happening, and what is going to happen. Are we moving into a dangerous new part of space, as our solar system moves around the galaxy? Is our very cellular structure evolving? What changes in our Akashic remembrance might be happening? Why now? All of these things are covered, as a reference to our new spiritual evolution.

Lee Carroll

Chapter Eight

"The Energy of the Future"

Kryon Live Channelling
Given in Newport, California

December 7, 2014

Greetings, dear ones, I am Kryon of Magnetic Service. This particular channelling will be filled with information, as it often is, but there is also something else that we offer. We're coming to the close of your calendar year 2014. It's normally a time for reflection and, in this particular room, the energy that we wish to generate with the entourage around you is that of congratulations. I want you to sit and bask in honor and, in these next moments, I would like you to try to disengage from the issues and the problems that you came with. As you sit there, if you have pain in your body – disengage. If you have pain in your heart – disengage. Corporeally, we understand fully that you are what you are, and you must go through what you go through, but you have the power to disengage from it for a while – for the next few moments. No matter what the message is to follow, or whatever is said, there is another energy that pervades the room. It sits and hovers over you, looks at you, remembers you, is thankful for you, and knows you. Even as we begin the information, we ask that the multiplicity of the messages going out be felt and understood and enjoyed to their fullest, within these moments.

The Premise of Cellular Evolution

If you are listening or reading this, and you are not in this physical meeting, we need to review something – a premise. There are some scientists and researchers who believe that the Human brain contains everything it ever could contain. That is to say, it contains genius, intelligence, manifestation over physics, and mastery in every single Human cell. But those attributes are locked away and, somehow, depending upon the chemistry and the energy that is multidimensional in every Human brain, there is a posturing of energy that keeps it locked out. The belief is that perhaps, at the right time, certain energies will come along and unlock it. This is the theory – that Humans are complete and developed and ready for everything.

Now, that theory opposes the other theory that tells you that the Human brain is not complete and it is a product of continuing and future cellular evolution to come. It says that you are no smarter than the full ability of the body to be smart. There's nothing in your body beyond what you see, and you will grow cells eventually to create a more evolved Human Being. Between these two theories, I will tell you that the former one is the accurate one. Evolution from now on will be energy based, not chemical based, and will unlock hidden wisdom and cellular efficiency – something that is already there and built-in.

Sometimes the proof of this premise comes in odd ways, dear ones, and you see it and you don't know what to make of it. A brain injury will cause an Akashic remembrance to be triggered, and an artist will spring up instantly where that Human was never an artist before. Sometimes something will happen, a hit on the head, a blow perhaps, where a genius will be produced where there was none before. These are the small evidences you have that perhaps the former theory is absolutely true, one that says, "Inside you is everything waiting to come out."

Take a look at spontaneous remission, for it's a puzzle, and some think it's a miracle. How could the body possibly instantly cure itself of some of the worst imbalances and diseases known to mankind? Yet, it happens repeatedly. So you come into the area of what we've been teaching, which is spiritual logic. Take a look at what I've said in the past: The old energy, which is on this planet now, has locked your DNA at approximately 33 percent to 34 percent. The long-lived and wise masters who walked on this planet had theirs at 80 percent to 90 percent. Everything they did was to show you what you could do. We have been teaching this over and over. Let this be the premise at which we begin.

The Physics of It: A Review

Now for some physics, and I'll call it spiritual physics so it's not too complicated. In 1993, we gave you a book called The End Times. In this book, we made some statements. We talked about the magnetic grid of the Earth, and we told you that it had to be there for Human life to exist – and it does. At the time, science didn't agree, but now, many are seeing it. We went on to give you the esoterics of it, what my partner calls the woo-woo part. Your DNA, a multidimensional molecule, has within it everything that the Universe knows. It carries your Akashic Record, all of your lifetimes, all of your spiritual purpose, your spiritual being and your karma. Everything is in your DNA. This will never be proven, since it's a spiritual attribute. The DNA creates a field and it's called the Merkabah (a Hebrew word).

We also told you that the magnetic grid of the Earth, a multi-dimensional energy, transfers certain things to your DNA on a day-by-day basis. The grid then becomes a major energy transfer system. That should have connected the dots for some of those who were paying attention – for if the grid changes, dear ones, you do, too. I told you the grid would change more in 10 years than it had in 100, and it did. You can measure your magnetic grid's movement with a compass. Between 1993 and 2002, it moved greatly, more than in any other time in modern Human history. We said this would be, and so it was. Our grid group left in 2002, as we told you we would.

Again, those paying attention should have known something was happening. I also told you within those initial transmissions back then that you would have no Armageddon, and you did not. Also, that there would be no World War III, and there wasn't. In the face of all the prophecy that told you differently, we told you there was a potential for Human Beings to pass the marker, survive, and start a new energy on the planet. We told you this would be the start of peace on Earth, and this is where you sit today. All of those years ago, we told you about the potential of where you sit today, listening to this message, and asking what might be next. So I'll label the channel right now: The Energy of the Future.

The Energy of the Future

Last week, I gave you a channelling of what to expect within the next three years. The message tonight will talk to you about the energies that are going to be manifested beyond that and some of the changes to expect and why they are taking place. You may want to listen to this channel a number of times to put it together, for there are reviews and new information.

So before we begin, what have we established?

Number One: Locked into the Human body via your DNA is brilliance and mastery, working at approximately 34 percent.

Number Two: The magnetic grid of the planet postures everything to do with your DNA. It also has much to do with what you call Human nature, what you want and what you've created. It seems static, never changing, and has been seen as "the way it is." However, we will call it the temporary lock on DNA. You see, when your Human consciousness and spiritual maturity starts to move in the next years, your DNA will start to change. This has nothing to do with chemistry, but everything to do with energy stored within it, and rewriting the data. New energies will unlock certain parts that have been locked, some of them being the very parts that I've just told you about at the beginning of this channelling – the things that are puzzling regarding healing and the Akash.

The Nodes and Nulls – Energies for the Future

Now, let's go a step further. Within the last two years, we told you about the opening of the nodes and the nulls, the time capsules of the planet that were waiting for this new energy. We told you who put them there, and that the Creative Source itself is responsible. We told you that they have been there for more than 100,000 years, waiting to be opened if you would pass the marker, and you just did. They are opening slowly, and we have identified them and have matched up some of the pairs for you. [www. monikamuranyi.com/extras/gaia-effect-extras/nodes-and-nulls/] They're beginning to open.

What do they do? I'll tell you. They pour out information onto the magnetic, Crystalline and Gaia grids – the three active interpersonal grids of this planet, the ones that interface between you and your consciousness. That's where their information goes. Isn't it interesting? The information does not go directly into your consciousness, but into the grids. Now, this allows for free choice, for it's not put into your mind. That would void free choice. Instead, it's put upon the grid. With free choice, any Human can ignore anything I'm saying and walk out of this room. He can say, *"The man in the chair is a fraud. The information is ridiculous; it's stupid!"* At the same time, sitting next to this doubter will be someone who is being miraculously healed this day. That's the difference. Free choice to accept or reject things around you is the key to honoring your individual consciousness.

The New Approaching Energy of Space

If you could see multidimensional energies, and you had the ability to stand back and watch your solar system as it raced around the middle of the galaxy, you could see a ribbon of energy that you are currently intersecting. Right now, your solar system, you might say, has been in a bubble of protective energy since life began on this planet. This is an astronomical measurement and is known by science. It even has a name. So this is not esoteric. As this bubble dissipates and you move into a new area of space, this ribbon of energy that you are now intersecting is different. In fact, it represents higher energy, and some might even call it radiation.

As your solar system moves firmly into it, it's the first time that this has ever occurred with Humans on the Earth. It takes millions of years for your solar system to make one revolution around the center [of the galaxy]. Therefore, you were not here the last time this took place. You are now sanctioned with the consciousness of the creative seed in you, and here comes the radiation, right on schedule. We have said this before and we have channelled this, for this is not new information. But now we put it together.

The first thing that this radiation intercepts is the largest thing in your solar system – your sun. The sun is a nuclear engine, and it has the most energy of your system. The new radiation interfaces with your sun and immediately the sun will change its energy. The sun will then blast this new information through the solar wind [the heliosphere of the sun] right to the Earth. It will immediately be intercepted by your magnetic grid [as normal], for your magnetic grid always intercepts any energy from the heliosphere. The heliosphere [the magnetic grid of the sun] overlaps the magnetic grid of the Earth, and the information transfer is complete through something called inductance. Now it's in your magnetic grid. As a review, remember that we have taught you that whatever attribute is in your magnetic grid is then transmitted to your DNA. Connect the dots from a 25-year-old message: The new energy affects the sun. The sun gives the energy to your grid, and your grid gives it to your DNA. You are affected.[1]

The New "Message" from Space

Let me tell you what the message is that is being communicated: Unlock to 44 percent! This is the message: The Human race has passed the marker and is ready for the next step in evolution. I am talking about the old soul. You are the ones who will be first to get this message. It is you, and some of your "old soul" children, who are starting to feel and accept this!

Let me tell you in this lesson today that the first thing that this unlocking will begin to create is what we're going to call Akashic acuity. You're going to start remembering, and it's about time. Can you celebrate this? It's about time that when you're born, you don't start from scratch, in the dark, and doing everything all over again. Instead, you remember!

I want to talk to some individuals who are listening to this and are in this room. Have your grandchildren had the audacity to tell you who they used to be? Don't raise your hand; I know you're here. They feel it, and they know it, and out of the mouths of these babes come the most profound information that this planet has ever heard! They knew who they were! Some will point their fingers at you and say, *"Don't you remember? I was your mum in another life."* That's a bit disconcerting, isn't it?

I want you to remember one of the premises of incarnation, the one that we have given you over and over. You incarnate in family groups. There's a reason for this, so there is comfort and joy. It's so you don't have to learn the energy of each related person, all over again, each time. The energies of the family stay together, and you can accomplish more that way. There's always a benevolent reason

---

for these things. Every single attribute of the esoteric system of life, whether it's your grids or reincarnation, is benevolent. Did you hear that? It's a beautiful system, and not random. It's not about judgment; it's not about punishment. It is, instead, about the love of God for you, and what I'm about to tell you is, what is changing is energy.

Akashic Acuity

So we have established that you are moving into this new radiation, and we have established that it intersects the sun. The sun blasts your magnetic field with it (via the solar wind) and the magnetic field talks to your DNA. Suddenly, there is the potential [that] some of your DNA is being unlocked. The attributes of unlocking Akashic acuity will help you to remember who you've been. Now, with this remembrance comes energy – not about who you were, but rather, it gives you the energy of what you did. I don't mean physically; I mean energetically and mentally. Old souls carry with them experience. When you look into the eyes of a child, you're going to see wisdom just waiting to break out. Dear ones, these children are different. They are not going to go through what you did! They have a whole new set of issues, and most of their issues are trying to navigate the old issues you create for them!

There's something we brought up in a former channelling called the wisdom factor. Now, the wisdom factor is caused by Akashic acuity. After living Human life over and over, you start remembering the wisdom that you have gained through these past lifetimes. You don't necessarily remember who you were, but rather, the fact that you were at all and the experiences you had. Imagine a child coming into the planet knowing how to read? Imagine a child coming into the planet knowing not to touch something hot? Where did it come from? You're going to see more of this, and a feeling of "been there, done that."

Akashic acuity is remembrance of experience during past lifetimes. As the child grows, that remembrance becomes pure wisdom.

As the child starts to awaken and the pineal opens, something else happens. The grid starts talking to the child through the DNA, and in the grid is also the information from the time capsules we spoke about in past channellings. The time capsules start feeding the planet with increased wisdom and knowledge. You don't have to reincarnate to awaken even further! Akashic acuity means suddenly Humans know more than other children have in the past – much more.

Fast Tracking

This is the plan, and it's a fast-track system, an energy system for planetary ascension. It's going to take a long time to implement, dear ones, but it's beginning right now. You're going to see marginal evidence of this beginning to happen in 2015, 2016, 2017. You're going to see it slightly in many places. These energies take a long time to mature, and they're not all going to happen fast and instantaneously. Some of you are going to be convinced that the world is going through a dark place and you're all going with it. This is because you don't see the changes for what they are, and you don't understand what is really happening. We've said it before, that when you shine a lot of light in a dark place, the things that were always in the dark object. That's what you're seeing now, and you'll see more of it. These dark things were always there, but they just didn't have the light on them that you're placing on them now.

Awareness of Self

Akashic acuity creates wisdom, and that wisdom translates into something else that we wish to tell you about. How do I present this case? When organisms become more complex, they work better. More cells together coalesce and communicate and work better. As you evolved as a life-force, systems became more elaborate and more mature. You ended up with the Human Being, who finally has what we would call sentience. That is to say, they are aware that you are here. I will give you another channelling soon that will actually explain the evolution of life on Earth. Cells of life reproduce, live, and consume energy that you haven't seen in science yet.

Awareness of self is one of the first attributes of spiritual intelligence, and here you sit with it. Today, you are much, much higher in evolvement than the animals just below you. You look into their eyes and you can see emotion and love, and you can see intelligence, but they don't know who they are, not really – not like you do. Your brain is the best one on the planet, and that happened because it got more complex, and systems worked together in ways you haven't figured out yet.

Now, why do I tell you this? This is because this basic truth is not reflected at all socially. Did you ever notice that the larger the organization, the more dysfunctional it becomes? Now, may I make the point to you that this is exactly the opposite from what has happened over time with cellular structure? There's something missing! The cells coordinate with each other in ways that you have not discovered yet. One knows what the other is doing, and there is a chemical and electrical balance that occurs. They all try to balance together. That's the beauty of a system that has coalescence and coherence. It puts together everything so that all have the same information and all work toward the same intelligent goal. How can you have trillions and trillions of cells in the Human body all working together, living for a long time, cooperating and doing their best to stay alive, yet you put several hundred people together and they're dysfunctional?

You know I'm right. The larger the social organization, the worse it works. Then you get into government. I don't have to tell you. It would appear in some cases that the organization is actually stupid, because there are too many of them trying to do the same thing. What is wrong with this picture? Let me show you this, because it's going to change.

Coalescing Consciousness

Here is a new phrase: Coalescing consciousness. Human Beings are going to start having the same kind of attributes of consciousness that your cells enjoy. They'll be connected. They will start to know what the other one is thinking. Not personally or privately, but intellectually and cooperatively. Common sense will be the guide. You'll find something very soon that you never thought could happen: Large organizations will start to function much better than they have [before]. We have even spoken about a day when there could be manager-less cooperation. This is all part of it, dear ones. Can you imagine a situation where no one is in charge? This can only happen if all of the individuals know the issues together. You see what I'm saying?

This, dear ones, is the wisdom factor. Can you imagine how this will affect everything? Let's start simply: Relationships, business in general, corporations, politics and governments. If consciousness is physics (as I have mentioned), that means there are absolute physical rules of wisdom, and that means it can be seen and worked with.

Do you remember that radiation that's coming your way in the solar system? Do you remember that it's going to hit the magnetic grid? All of this is going to start unlocking your DNA. It will only unlock what you have free choice to accept, dear ones. It won't happen to you unless you give permission for it. My job is to tell you to watch for it!

You're all coming back, and I've told you this. Regardless of what your tired body says now, you are returning. Imagine a young body with the knowledge that you gained this time around, where you won't have to make the same mistakes! You will be coming in fresh, looking good, and remembering! You're not going to miss this party, dear ones. Every single time when I've seen you on my side of the veil, you can hardly wait to go at it again, especially if there's some redemption coming. You've spent a lot of time fighting the old energy, dear ones. Now, why not enjoy what you've paid for and earned? There's more.

The Playground, Again

We told you last week that the metaphor of all of this is the children in the playground. Can you remember what it was like in the playground? Do you remember the bullies? Do you remember feeling inadequate or maybe you were a bully? You may have acted out whatever it was you did in your juvenile consciousness, and other children did the same. It was survival, and you did whatever you could to hold your own.

But this changed as you grew up, and as young adults, you didn't do playground things anymore. You didn't tease or throw rocks or call names. Now you knew better, because you had grown up and were wiser. Now, think of a humanity that never got out of the playground until now. In this new post-2012 energy, you are given the tools of the maturity that you've earned. You see civilization with new eyes, and the playground starts to disappear. Wisdom begins to figure it out.

Dear ones, you're not going to have humanity go into this new wisdom as long as they are warring barbarians. By the way, that's all you've done through eons! You've learned how to kill each other better and better through the years, and suddenly the consciousness is changing. Humans are starting to realize on a grand scale that *this is not what we want.* Oh, believe me, there's going to be continuous argument with that, but slowly, the majority will have this realization.

Just as in real life, you realize some of the bullies never grew up and are still playing by "playground rules." You're seeing some of them on the planet right now. They would love to take the old, dark energy and put it right back where it was before 2012. They would love to make you afraid, but it's not going to happen. Wisdom is changing.

Your Innate is going to start changing. Innate is the smart body intelligence (that's the energy you muscle test to communicate with). The bridge between the corporeal and the Innate is missing, and it's going to start being constructed. Let me put this in simple terms. You will eventually be your own medical intuitive. You'll know what's going on in every organ in your body and in every gland – you'll know if there's balance in your blood! Don't you think your brain should let you know that? Your Innate already knows it! It's always trying to balance itself, and the only thing it left out is your consciousness! Does this current system sound complete to you? It's not working well. But when you start operating at 44 percent, this becomes a reality. This is just the beginning, dear ones.

Imagine a Human Being who would know these things. You may look at them and say they are a super-person. How can they have that? Welcome to the future! Peace on Earth is just the beginning and it's a no-brainer, as my partner would say, because it automatically comes with wisdom. You stopped beating each other up on the playground when you got to be an adult. You developed a maturity and a little bit of elegance. Your agenda changed, and you had to get along.

That's what we are looking at for this planet! That's our prediction. It's not immediate, but it starts now. We are giving you the ABCs of how this works, so that it will be real to you when it happens. This explanation is so you will understand it's not a magic potion of energy that's going to sweep over the Earth and cause peace. It's not. The engine of it comes from your DNA, your wisdom, your incarnations and with what you decide to do. That's the message. It's work!

Now, there are always those who would say *"How soon? It all sounds so good."* I want you to remember: Some of you were here 20 years ago when my partner brought me to a room very similar to this and for the first time he allowed me to open up and give you messages. At that point in time, we gave you information that is now right in front of you, happening. We saw the potentials of what would be and what you would do. It was not a wasted prophecy, for it happened!

Spirit does not know the future, for that's free choice of humanity. But we know the patterns that have happened before on other planets. We've seen what you're doing now, and we've seen an overview that no Human Being can see. We know what's going on in the cracks. We see things you wouldn't believe, all of which are pushing you forward. How soon? This is up to you. There are so many things in your favor, and this includes that which is happing in your solar system, which is on schedule for the new Human.

The precession of the equinoxes and the end of 2012 marked the beginning of a Human consciousness that starts to go into maturity. This was the prophecy of the Ancients. Next, there is an age of getting used to it. I'm not going to tell you how long that's going to last. On other planets, it was amazingly short. The potential is there for you to get through this quickly. Dear ones, you have paid the price for this. All of the lifetimes of working this puzzle have culminated to this point, and now you are having the freedom to see the end of it. It takes adjustment to move from the old to the new, and in the adjustment a recalibration of finding a new frequency is upon you. Getting out of fear is upon you.

Finally, I will say to you something that I have said before, and I want you to hear it again and again. The reason for repetition is so you will understand what you see. The darkness will try to win now that the light has been turned on. They have one tool, which is potent – really potent. This tool can get to the highest of the high and ruin them. It can get to the Lightworker, the healer and the channeller. It's a four-letter word called fear. If you're afraid, then they have won. I want you to think about that. They know this. Let your light shine through this in such an amazing way that there is no longer a horrible, controlling four-letter word. It doesn't even exist. March through these times and remember them, for you expected them and worked toward them. Work toward the new four-letter word – LOVE.

Stay a moment and celebrate each other.

And so it is.

Chapter Nine

Israel

Never in my life have I had an experience like what happened to me in Israel in 2015. Here are thirteen channellings, given in thirteen locations in this small and historic country of Israel. I was continually overwhelmed with emotion, as I gave these short channellings in some of the most profound spiritual places that are still available to be visited. The history and spiritual significance of the Shift was overwhelming to me in each location.

We took 300 people on this special tour, and I would love for you to see the accompanying thirty-minute video that I made, which documented the places where we channelled, and where you can actually hear a few lines of the channellings. [**www.kryon.com/israelvideo**].

Each of the thirteen channellings are titled with a word starting with a specific letter of the alphabet. When Kryon does this, the letters always spell something significant. In this case, you may have a difficult time deciphering what the phrase is that Kryon is spelling with the thirteen letters (in the order that the channels were given), since he is spelling the words BACKWARDS! In honor of the languages of the land (Hebrew and Arabic), Kryon gave us a profound message. Using each letter, go ahead and rearrange them into the phrase that is spelled correctly in English, so you can participate in the overall message of this tour.

Lee Carroll

Chapter Nine

"Israel"

Kryon Live Channellings
13 channels given during Kryon Israel Tour

September 30 - October 6, 2015

Each of these channellings was centered around an alphabetic letter in English. Kryon has done this on several other occasions. The thirteen given letters in this channelling spell: LEARSI NI ECAEP. Only part way into the tour did an Israeli attendee figure out what this meant. It is actually PEACE IN ISRAEL spelled backwards. The backwards spelling is in honor of the languages of the region (Hebrew and Arabic), which are written from right to left.

Highlights of this entire Israel tour can be seen in a profoundly moving 30-minute video at [www.kryon.com/israelvideo].

The Letter L (LIVING TRUTH)

Given at El-Burak Steps, The Temple Mount, Old City Jerusalem – Wednesday morning, September 30, 2015

Greetings, dear ones, I am Kryon of Magnetic Service. I know where I am, and I know where you are. There will be many, many listeners who are not really aware of where you all sit today. The series of channels for these days, like so many adventures that we go on together, will each have a letter to guide them. At the end of the series the letters will all spell something profound. The letter today is "L."

Dear ones, you sit in an historic place [referring to "The Temple Mount" – seated at El-Burak Steps]. We don't have to tell you anything about it, for it is well known. All the Masters of this land walked in this area. This letter "L" today is going to be about you. It's going to be about "LIVING TRUTH." It's not about Israel; not about the Masters; not about the stones that you sit on, or about the masses that gather behind you [referring to the thousands of pilgrims celebrating their big yearly Jewish holiday called Sukkot or "The Feast of the Tabernacles"]. It's about you.

Not all of you are here to hear these words from Kryon. I know who is here. Many are here to simply enjoy the history and ponder the energy. But there are so many listening, who join in this moment [speaking of the vast online listenership for the audios]. I want to ask you if you are living the truth that you believe. What really brings you to this place? This is about you, dear ones. Before any other messages about Israel are given, or what might have happened here, you must suspend all things and consider your own process. Do you believe there is God inside?

I want you to think for a moment of what has occurred within the consciousness of the Masters who walked this area. They had God inside. Some of them had direct communications, and they told you so. *We believe in one benevolent creator.* This is what was taught, and this never changed. God is the same then, as today, and forever. God is inside you. Can you take that information and build something with it? Can you then project this God energy from you to the world? When you look around you, do you see things in your filter, your culture, or do you see God inside of all that you witness? When you see these lands and gaze upon the past, what occurs to you? Were you here? Or if not, were you at least alive somewhere else? And if not, do you relate to the Creative Source that is here? In our next channel, we will remind you of what this really represents, but for now, "L" is for "Living Your Truth."

Even as you arise in a moment from where you sit, and you look upon those who are worshiping in their cultural way, you will see the many kinds of doctrines, beliefs, rules, and protocol. You will see the beauty of their clothing, and the honor they see in how they present themselves before their God. They're serious, dear ones, and they're living their truth. What about you? You are here to plant the seeds of the consciousness of a New Earth. The City on the Hill is where you are! This is, and always has been, the symbol of a New Jerusalem. It's a place that will represent peace, not a harsh situation. What is your truth today? Do you believe it? Can you believe it? Can it be true with what you see here?

Before you can do anything else here, and before you hear any other channelling on this tour, that's the message of today. Can you see what is here and understand what we are saying? What is your truth today? Where are you with that, dear Human Being?

And so it is we start the journey, and so it is that the next channel will feature another letter. But let this letter now be first and foremost – Live Your Truth these days, and therefore see what is here with more mature eyes.

And so it is.

The Letter E (ENERGY of the Region)

Given in the Garden of the Tower of David, Old City Jerusalem – Wednesday afternoon, September 30, 2015

Greetings, dear ones, I am Kryon of Magnetic Service. Again, I will state that there is no question of where I am or what has happened this day. There is also no question about what is being experienced by many, even now. To say it is beautiful is a vast understatement. Today you have seen what many never will see [speaking of the tens of thousands worshiping at the Western Wall for the festival of Sukkot]. There is something special, is there not, in watching Human Beings speak in their way to the Creative Source? It's profound to have such dedication, which is life-long, about that which they believe about the One God. Their God is a historic God, who is beautiful to them and to you.

We continue with the series of letters, and the theme will be an "E." It's going to stand for the "ENERGY of the Region." Now, I want to be careful here, so that you understand where I am going in this discussion. What I am going to speak of briefly is different from what you might think. I didn't say the energy of Israel, for the borders here have changed over time, and that is what you have learned earlier today. You have now heard the stories of who conquered whom, when, and what happened. You have seen the history of the many temples, and have seen what is left. That's all about Human history.

I want to talk about the region and what occurred here. I want to talk about the Israelites, the historic Jews, and what really happened here. I want to talk about Abraham and what happened in the region. If you will look at some of the sayings that you may have heard, both in scripture and also from the wisest of people who are outside of scripture, they have used the word "chosen" when they speak of the Jews. I'm going to tell you what this means, and it might be different than you have been told.

Are the Jews "The Chosen People?" Indeed they are, but chosen for what? It's not what you have been told; for the Jews were chosen to give the Earth something it didn't have. They did, and it happened right here in this region. The Jews brought together the philosophies of this planet and they found the One God, and they were chosen for this task. Right now on this planet, you have what you would call a monotheistic Earth. This is entirely due to what happened in the region. I want you to think of this for a moment, and the changes that occurred because of this.

So the Jews gave Earth the divine principle of the One God and it spread around the globe. For this message, they have paid dearly in so many ways, and many in the region have paid along with them. Let me ask you, where are you from? What did your parents believe in? What did you believe? Are there many Gods, or one? All over the lands that you came from geographically [speaking to the 300 attendees], there is, indeed, the belief in one God. It happened because of what took place in this region.

So "The Chosen Ones" were chosen to give the planet a unity that the planet continues to believe and enjoy to this day. That unity is the oneness of Spirit. I speak to you from the Creative Source, to a monotheistic Earth because of the events in this very place. The lineage of Abraham is what we celebrate, which became the lineage, really, of the planet, spiritually, and that's what I want to tell you about – perhaps a little differently than you think.

With this message, came the creation of strife for all those in the area, and it has lasted for years and years – even to this day. There are religious wars over how the One God should be worshiped, and who the One God would look upon with favor. These arguments became the issue. But the Jews were chosen to give the Earth a unification principle, even though it stirred the pot of Human Spirituality.

This oneness that was given then, now has an opportunity to expand and mature. This, again, falls upon the Chosen, and you're going to hear me talk about this more when the time is right. Those who listen to (and read) this now may understand what this means at this time in history. The new energy past 2012 was prophesied to create a new kind of unity between Humans. It will take time to grow up within this energy, and to mature within this new energy, and to have the belief systems morph within it.

But the Chosen, the lineage of Abraham, will then be tasked with creating the "rest of the story." They will be the ones to create a unity within their land, with their enemies within and outside of their borders. Again, they will give this planet something it needs. Who better to do this, than the ones who gave us the One God? They are the ones who must do it. They're postured for it, and they're ready for it. They must unite those around them for a real Peace on Earth. How can this possibly be done? How can anyone change things as you see them here? How can you deal with the walls that are here, the differences, the frustrations, the history?

There will come a time, dear ones, when this land, which has been the same for thousands of years, will actually move off of sameness and you will see breakthroughs in consciousness. They will be small, but you will see the beginning of compassion, one with another, and although it will be small, it will grow. The idea of borders being open because of trust, which has never happened, will happen. When? What will be the catalyst for this? How can it change? Those answers will come partially because you're here, dear ones. This week you are planting the seeds of a new consciousness. Indeed you're learning about the Chosen – not what they did, but what they are chosen to do.

This is the new task of the Israelis and the Israelites – new and old, and this is what we have now said for twenty-six years. We sit here now, and we make the statement once again in this new energy: "As go the Jews, goes Earth." Listen to that. What are you going to do with it? I want you to take that message home and to every single one who you meet in this land, I want you to take these people home in your heart, and honor them for the task they must do. I want you to remember the faces. I want you to remember the regalia and the ceremony. It may not be what you thought it would look like here, or what you would choose for your own spiritual path, but I want you to remember the compassion that they have for their God. Dear ones, it's going to start shifting into the compassion they have for humanity, and their God.

God is within you. This is Letter E.

And so it is.

_____

The Letter A (ASSIMILATION)

Given in Masada – Thursday morning, October 1, 2015

Greetings, dear ones, I am KRYON of Magnetic Service. I know where I am, and for those listening, we are in Masada in Israel. If you don't know what happened here in history, you should find out. For Masada is profound history for the Jews in this land. It is more than profound, for it sets the attitude of the civilization living here. I'm going to reveal some things here. Some items may be controversial, and some may not agree with what historians have told you.

We're going to examine the letter "A" today, and it will stand for "ASSIMILATION." Before I do this, I have a history of revealing specific and profound Human history and will do it yet again today. All you can do is read about it here, since none of you were there. Spirit was! We saw humanity within a lower energy of survival, and we watched the Jews right here. I have revealed history in the past that has been controversial. I did it in Bolivia not too long ago within a historical site thousands of years old. Those digging could not figure out why they found artifacts that did not belong. They made assumptions that were completely and totally wrong, and in my channelled message, I reminded them that no matter what the society, no matter how old, they had museums of their own. The archaeologists had cracked into the historical site's museum! There they found things from other places. This is typical of any museum anywhere. Even the ancients honored their ancestors and their past. Let those who study archaeology be aware that not everything is as it seems simply because it's in one strata or layer in the dirt. Not everything is as it seems here, either.

Masada

Oh, the stories are accurate and the basics are well known about this historic place. There are heroes here, much courage, and assimilation. Let me tell you what happened – a story within the story. The overlay of what you should know about this grand story will give enhancement to the known story. It gives it pure glory, and a splendor that you might not appreciate: These were Jews, and on this mountaintop they all knew something: They had assimilated the truth of the lineage of Abraham. They knew about the One God, and they knew of their own history. They knew of the One God that could be spoken to, and the One God who they could receive commandments from. They knew the reality of what happens after life – they knew it. The Romans had nothing. This was before a monotheistic planet. The Romans had their God and it was a dysfunctional Human! The Romans didn't know what the Israelites knew.

I want you to think for a moment of how this would affect you if you had to have made the choices that were made on this mountaintop. I want you to know something: The ten who were left, after they had killed their own families, were not in sorrow. Oh, they were pensive for what had happened, but they absolutely knew what was next for them and their slain loved ones. They were Jews with the lineage of Abraham. They had assimilated the truth and it rang in every cell of their bodies.

I want to tell you something that is honoring, but that may be controversial. The decision was made here for all to perish, and it was made by warriors, not the women or the children. In the final meetings of men only, the women and the children had no idea what was next and what the plans would be. As always, they had turned to their leaders to find out what the strategy would be. The men who were warriors came out of the final decision meeting and they had already decided on the timing of the death of their families. It would be quick and without anxiety. It would happen all over the mountain top, at the same time, and before sundown. The vast Roman army, that had camped out for months below them, had built a ramp and was about to breach the walls of the city.

Each man killed his wife first, quickly and by surprise. She would not feel it coming. They did it by the blade, so that the woman would have no idea that the children were next. Do you understand this? There was honor in their system. Only for a second or two would there be pain, and then they would be with the One God. The men knew it. They had assimilated a basic truth of life and death, and the glory of God. It wasn't a painful sacrifice for them, for all ten knew that, before long, they would also be with their families. This was their assimilation of the truth of the One God and the afterlife.

Think of it. Although it may have been painful for their hearts at the moment, there was joy in what they had decided. There would be no slavery or suffering from the Roman soldiers who were about to breach the community. There would be no violation of their precious wives, and the women would not be subject to knowing about the children … ever. The children were next: quickly, as warriors, they knew how to do it very fast, and yes, there was the pain of the heart, but you didn't hear wailing from the houses, as the movies perhaps would show you. It was done with honor and silence. There was serenity, knowing about the love of God and the lineage of Abraham – and the Romans didn't have a clue. The men came together and began to deal, one by one, with each other in the same way ... until the end.

When the Romans arrived, the smell of victory was robbed from them. They had no idea this could happen. It was a shock to see how many had decided to be with the One God, instead of being taken by the soldiers. What you also didn't know was that many of the Roman soldiers wept when nobody was looking. For they somehow knew that they had not gained anything, and had somehow missed something profound within their own lives.

That's what happened here, and you can take that information and you can cry. You can have sorrow about the three-dimensional aspect of it all, but I want you to relax in the arms of Spirit right now and see the beauty of the plan. I want you to see the honor in which it was carried out, and the love of God which they all experienced within this quick death. I want you to see this place differently than perhaps you were told.

That's enough for now. Assimilation. Can you assimilate your belief to the same degree they did? Oh, ones of a monotheistic planet, again I say, it started here!

And so it is.

The Letter R (REMEMBER)

Given in Mitzpe Gilgal – Thursday afternoon, October 1, 2015

Greetings, dear ones, I am Kryon of Magnetic Service. We've waited a long time to give you this channel, and for over two decades we have spoken of it in pieces and in parts. Now we sit in a place where we can honor it in a different way.

The letter for this channel is "R" and it stands for "REMEMBER." Now, if you were not here when the prophet Elijah ascended, how would you remember it? The answer is that all of you have profound Human history at some level within your Akash. Now, we have not said this before in this way. The Human Akash is extremely complex, and it is related and inter-related with other Humans, other souls, and time itself. You might say there are layers of Akashic remembrance. There is Individual soul remembrance, and planetary remembrance – an attribute that would be related to the energy of Gaia.

Some of you have actually started to awaken to the potential that you might have been here in this area in the past. Not all of you, but it always happens when we bring many people to an area or a place that has this energy. There would be a resounding remembrance to a past energy, and many might feel it. I want you all to remember something that happened very close to here, and we're going to speak yet again of Elijah. For two decades, I have spoken of Elijah, and it's not because of his Jewish lineage. Rather, it's because of the lesson that he showed to the planet about the One God.

Picture for a moment what happened here. Of all the times that I have spoken of this story, it is more real today than ever before. For, now you sit upon the land, very close to where the ascension occurred. Think for a moment of a very wise Master. Elijah did many great things and he, indeed, was wise, and God knew him. The man who was his understudy, and who was going to some day take his mantle, was called Elisha. We use the word mantle to represent all that was Elijah – his knowledge, and his wisdom. Think of it almost like a cloak, or a coat that one would take off and put on another Human when he passes. You will find this full story in the Old Testament, written down for the event that happened not too far from here. You might say that the Holy Scriptures are really often a history of a people. The story is in that scripture which you would call Second Kings, and it's a familiar story from Kryon.

Elijah knew that his time was up, but he also knew at his level of vibration [as a Master], that he would not pass through death. You might wonder to yourself, *"Are these things accurate and true? For, no Human is recorded to have done this again since Elijah."* The true answer is that it, indeed, has been done, but not recorded. We often get into these kinds of teachings about those early times, and we explain that, in those early days, there were Masters on this planet who vibrated much, much higher than you do now. This actually was the reason for seeing them as Masters at all. Some of them lived very long lives due to this. It led all the way to that which you would call the Master Christ [who was also of the lineage of Abraham].

High vibrating Masters needed to be in these lands. They had to exist in this way, for they were examples of a loving God, one who communicates, and one who is real and cares about each soul. This was so different from what humanity actually thought at the time. Many Gods were often the way Humans saw creation, and as we have told you, the Jews brought the message of Monotheism to the planet.

Elijah was one of those Masters, and vibrated at a very high level. He knew he could control the time he left the Earth, and he knew when it was time to go. How it exactly took place is Elijah's business, but he knew it and he knew it enough in advance that he told Elisha to get ready to watch it and write down what he saw. I have told the story many times, and it's an accurate and true one. However, it also involves Human nature, Human perception, and a truth that we teach that Elijah showed us by having Elisha watch.

It was time, and Elijah told Elisha to get ready to say goodbye and to watch this process and write it down. Elijah told him: *"I have chosen my time of departure and I'm going to ascend."* As the story goes, Elijah literally walked out into the dirt and ascended. It's the very dirt you stand on, the dirt you sit on, the dirt that is here today. Think of it! You are here where it happened!

Elijah stood there for some time, and then something miraculous happened: He started to transform and prepare to ascend. This is where a question is often asked: *"At what point did God come down to collect Elijah? Was it now?"* The answer is no. So we continue: According to the writings of Elisha, he watched with open eyes as multidimensional things took place before him – multidimensional, because what he saw was not in 3D. This is the way Humans all see or perceive a divine energy. Even the burning bush [the story of Moses] was a manifestation of the perception of Human 3D. It was a bush that was on fire, but that did not consume itself. It was more than a bush. Some say, it had an angelic form or a voice, but it was never in 3D.

The transformation began, and if you want to know what took place, at what point it took place, I don't even think that Elisha knew the significance of what he saw, but he took it all in and watched it unfold. The first thing he saw was light. It was a light so bright he had never seen anything like it, and it actually hurt his eyes. The light took place around Elijah on the ground where Elijah was standing.

Question (second time): *"Is this the time that God came down and got Elijah?"* The answer is no. The story goes on, for in the perception of Elisha, he started to see shapes and even things that we can now tell you have numerological meanings. One of the things that he saw was a wheel. He didn't just see a wheel. He saw a wheel within a wheel. Now, this was his multidimensional perception, for there was no wheel, but it was being shown to Elisha that he might figure it out later.

It's important to tell you that the historical Jewish prophet Ezekiel also saw a wheel, and for the same reasons. It's actually a little-known event that Elisha also saw it, and not in all the stories. However, I was there. The meaning: The circle or the shape of the circle is the perfect shape and you will find it all through that which is spiritual history. It is also the shape of the halo. The larger circle that he saw represented the unending love and purity of God. There is no beginning and there is no end to a perfect circle. But Elisha saw two circles. One was within the larger one. The one within, represented the Human Being's Soul, and it was a never-ending circle with no beginning and no end – just like your own soul.

Slightly smaller than the big circle which encompassed it, the inside circle became one with the larger one. One with the other, the now single unit started to morph into something else, and Elisha said it looked like a chariot with wheels. It was the illusion of a chariot drawn by three white horses. You have to understand the numerology of the three. Three in ancient times represented a catalytic energy. A catalyst is something that is always changing things around it. With three white horses and a chariot, it meant that Elijah was about to ride somewhere. Elisha named the chariot with Elijah in it – Merkaba. Now, that means "to ride" in Hebrew. "The chariot of ascension" was then identified as the Merkaba for all humanity to understand. With Elijah's ascension, Elisha was identifying the Human Being's sacred spiritual "print" – the multidimensionality of the sacredness of the Human Being as seen in 3D. He was seeing Elijah's sacred parts unfold right before his eyes.

For the third time I will ask: Is it time yet for the almighty God, the Creator of the Universe, to finally come down and get him? And the answer is no, for what Elisha saw next was the chariot and all with it, ascending together! He watched his master, Elijah, disappear into the sky. The final lesson therefore, and the most important one, the one that I have been telling you for over twenty years now, is that you are God. God didn't have to come down and get Elijah, because God was in Elijah! The energy that Elijah had was strong and sacred enough to carry him into the heavens.

It's you in you, dear ones. The energy of the Creator is inside. It's not what God does for you, or with you, or to you. You have

God inside! Your ascension, that time of passing for every single Human, is the same. You leave on your own and you ascend on your own. This was the greatest lesson of the Master Elijah, given not too far from here. The whole idea of the Merkaba was presented, and it also showed the numerology of the changing Human soul.

The three is a representation of the fact that the soul returns. It's always changing. It doesn't go someplace and stay there, any more than your relationship with God does. It is always changing. Your spiritual relationship changes as you change. The God of Abraham is still the same energy today, but the relationship God had with Abraham has changed greatly to the relationship that you have with God today. This is the change! This is the catalyst, and the three represented by the horses that carried the Merkaba.

I've waited a long time to sit where all this happened, and to finally reveal some of the metaphors that are so beautiful, which Elijah showed. Elisha wrote it with such clarity that we could give you this information so many years later. Sit and honor this story, for it happened not too far from here. Same God, same dirt, same place. Think on these things; it's beautiful.

And so it is.

_____

The Letter S (SOUL)

Given on the Sea of Galilee – Friday morning, October 2, 2015

Greetings, dear ones, I am Kryon of Magnetic Service. For those listening (and reading), we are all together, floating on the Sea of Galilee. It is a beautiful place filled with the kind of history that is all over this land. Indeed, it would seem that you cannot take a step very far in this land before you literally find yourself in some kind of historic place.

The Masters walked this place, so many of them, and they all taught the One God. You have heard us talk about this over and over. In this message we have a letter for you, and we have some teaching. Oh yes, it will be very controversial. The letter is "S" and S will stand for the "SOUL."

We're going to reveal some things we have not spoken of before. For many years, we have waited to present information in an area where it happened. There is another attribute that is present, as well: None of you right now are grounded [referring to being on the water]. This creates something different for your perception, your consciousness of spirituality, and even this teaching. Things happen on the water. Look at that which you call scripture: How many things happened on the water? Many. And this is not just a metaphor for when you float, for you are not connected to[touching] the land. So because of those differences, we're going to teach now about the soul.

The soul is probably one of the most complex subjects we could ever discuss. First, it is not linear. Now, what we mean by that is this: A linear mind, as a Human has, tends to have a thought process that works in a straight line. Logic is this way, survival is this way, and business is this way. You live your lives day-by-day, by using consciousness, which is for the most part, linear. When you become even slightly multidimensional, that's when you start having the kinds of non-linear visions using metaphors that you're studying in this very land. The soul is a multidimensional part of the Human Being. It carries the piece of God that is, literally, the essence of God. In the soul, there are also the attributes of the Akashic record of every Human Being. When you pass away corporeally, the soul leaves the physical body. You go from being partly multidimensional, partly 3D, to fully multidimensional. You saw that in our message regarding Elijah. Now, here is where many belief systems vary. Some systems have the soul as a part that never returns to the planet. Some have the soul going into judgment, and the judgment would then send the soul one place, then another, and even perhaps another, like a stair-step of punishment or reward. But what was the original Human intuition about God within organized spiritual systems on the planet? Before there were ever doctrines and rules and structure, what was the original intuitive thought? We are looking at "pristine Human first intuition" about the Creator.

Let us go back more than 9,000 years. What was the initial thinking? At the time when there were many God potentials, a time, literally, before the Jews put it together and gave the Earth a monotheistic, beautiful Creator – what was the original thought about the soul? The Hindus and the Buddhists will disagree about who was actually first. But what both groups believed was this: The soul is forever, and it comes and goes from this planet in a circle. They felt there was a reason for this – a system – and they may even have called it "lessons." They taught that, the more Human Beings visited the Earth through reincarnating the soul, the more they learned. When they come back again, they have something called past life energy or karma and continue a path that often lasts eons and eons. Dear ones, everything you are hearing is simply returning to that original belief! This is the way of it. What has happened since then is mostly what men have done with it, not a change in God's plan.

Most of you feel that you have lived before. Some of you are even relating to the dirt of the Earth when you walk in this land. You're not on it right now, so you can relate to it differently: You reflect. Water is a reflective energy, so it's time to reflect on who you've been. Now, here is the reason for this entire lesson: There are several things we wish to tell you about the soul which we have told you before, and one thing we have never told you.

The soul carries your Akash [record of lifetimes]. When you come back to the planet, the Akash comes with you [is picked up when you arrive again]. No matter what culture, no matter who you are, no matter what gender, the Akash past-life record is part of you. We have stated before, that this is complex, for it's not always just your chemical lineage. For instance, you can have one chemical lineage with your parents, yet another Akashic lineage from another land. We're not going to dwell on that, for it's a conundrum for a logical mind. Instead, we're going to dwell on something else: Your soul inside you is always connected to God. We spoke yesterday of Elijah. What you saw in studying his ascension was an exposure to the grandness of his soul. Elisha reported some shapes and we told you that. We also told you that the prophet Ezekiel saw these same shapes again later. The shapes are common and they mean the same thing: They are the circle and represent the purity of the soul, and the circle of return.

Twenty-six years ago we made a statement. The statement is controversial. It was not understood then, and it is not understood now. Here it is: The soul of the pure Jew does not reincarnate as anything but a Jew. Now, there are many who will say, *"Well, that's just what Kryon says. It couldn't be true."* Let me reveal something: The soul of the Jew does not reincarnate as anything but a Jew! It is the only culture, the only lineage, which has this attribute – and here is how it works.

If you have the pure lineage, that is to say, a Jewish Akash in every cell, not part, you have reincarnated again and again and again as a Jew. There isn't any other group, whether it's cultural or race or belief, that has this purely Akashic attribute. When we first said this truth, many walked away from Kryon. There is a huge bias, as well, and many said, *"This cannot be so, for there is no reason."* Oh yes, there is!

I want you to use your spiritual logic with me for a moment. Drop your bias and linear thinking. Use the same logic of the Hindu.

If you come into any kind of school and you learn and you learn and you learn, you start to go up the ladder of knowledge, and retention of maturity and experience. The longer you attend a single school, and the one course study, the more proficient you are at what you're learning. The Jews had to have this lineage to bring the world a monotheistic God! This is the attribute that allowed them to stay in the same attributes of the Akash.

When they were born back on Earth, literally their consciousness would awaken at some level and say, *"Here I am again."* It's the same language, the same culture, the same laws, the same rules, over and over and over. They became very good at what they did. Is there any question why there are billions and billions of people on this planet who have a belief system which came right from here? [Jewish – Christian – Muslim]. A special kind of Human was needed in a special group to put it together and give this information to the planet the way they did. It also isolated them, and has made them different in perception to many cultures. Listen, they have paid the price for being different, but they are good at what they do. Is it inappropriate for you to look around the planet and see the "elephant under the table"? Jews run the largest organizations in business. They know what they are doing. They've been there, they've done that, and they reincarnate yet again and learn more. If you really want to be inappropriate, they are the ones who put the "Jew" in jewelry! They control this, too! You can shut your eyes and ignore all this, within your bias. You can resent the fact that they are so good at this, but you can't ignore the truth: They know what they're doing on Earth, like no other group. Perhaps now, you also realize why the fundamentalist Jews must marry into pure Jewish lineages? This truth is in their very DNA!

Now you also understand more about why this is the only lineage on the planet that has had the specter of genocide, or slavery en masse. From the ancient Egyptians to the modern wars ... if you could stop the Jewish lineage, you would stop the major plan of the One God – eventual peace on Earth. The bias remains, and old, dark energy on this planet right now would still love to stop it all.

Now, here is what I've never said before, regarding the soul of the Jew: It's going to take a special kind of an Akashic Human Being to create peace on Earth. The shift of energy that was expected is here. It affects all humanity. It affects consciousness. The precession of the equinoxes was not just a date. The Mayan calendar was correct: A new energy is upon you. The Nodes and Nulls are delivering new information to the planet right now. Consciousness is starting to change, and you'll see it first in the young people; and dear ones, the young Jews are different. They have a pure Akash, and thousands and thousands of lifetimes of being in the same culture has given them something new in this energy.

The same Akashic maturity of the Jews that brought together the planet and taught humanity about One God, is the same attribute and talent that must organize humanity for peace.

This is their task! It would seem unbelievable, as you look around, that such a thing could come from here. There is such diversity, such frustration, and so many belief systems. This is why they need that which they have – the ability to multi-task, to organize, to pull together. It's going to come from here!

This is the prophecy I will give you today: There is no other group who can do this. This is the one. It started here, and it's going to continue with solution here. You will see! People will ask, *"Kryon, is it going to happen in my lifetime?"* Of course, you will be here, but perhaps not in this corporeal lifetime – but you will be here! However, it's happening even now. Watch social media. The enemies that surround Israel are starting to change, and what is starting to change is not in their seniors, but it's within their children. The young people are going to create a brand new kind of association between countries. I used a different word, because the paradigms of peace are going to start shifting with new ideas of what can happen. How can you put together so many things that are so unequal in so many ways? You sit and say, *"Impossible! It cannot be done. We have tried for years!"* How many times in history have you seen impossible things change due to a change in thinking? The Akash will lead the way. It's time. The young people will be doing it, led by the Jews, who will know intuitively how to bring together things that can't be brought together.

That is today's message, as you float upon the Sea of Galilee.

And so it is.

The Letter I (I AM THAT I AM)

Given on the Mount of Beatitudes
– Friday afternoon, October 2, 2015

Greetings, dear ones, I am Kryon of Magnetic Service. We sit on the Mount of Beatitudes. You might hear the wind blowing in the background. It's a beautiful end of a powerful day, and the trees sing in joy to be in this place. Much has already been said, even before I begin, about the blessessednesses of the Human Being [The Beatitudes in Scripture], and the many things and concepts presented in this place are modern ones. These concepts live in this day, in their truth.

This channel today is not going to be lengthy. It's not a channel of great information, and it's not even all that new. Instead, we just want you to feel it. Energy is being delivered to all of you, right now. The kind of energy depends upon what the attitude is of the receiver. Does this place mean anything to you? When you leave this place, will you be different in any way? Is it simply the end of another tour day, or is there more? What happened here, or metaphorically here, is what we speak of. But that's not what this channel is about.

We're going to briefly examine another letter. The letter is "I." It is the last letter in a word, and the word is now complete. In the thirteen channels in this tour, there will be three words, and the "I" which we wish to examine now is part of a statement. Here is the statement: "I AM THAT I AM." When my partner first heard this as a child, he closed his eyes and asked his mother, *"Is that English?"* It is nonsense in English, for the word AM is normally followed by something else – a condition: I am tired. I am happy. I am joyful. I am hot. But, I AM THAT I AM, makes no sense.

As my partner grew up and became an adult, he heard the phrase over and over in spiritual circles, but it didn't get any better. Now as an adult, his son asked him, *"Dad what does that mean?"* Of course, he mustered all the wisdom that he had and delivered the answer: *"God works in mysterious words."* [Laughter] Dear ones, naturally, it meant more in the language that it was delivered. There are words and concepts in other languages that do not exist in my partner's speech, or even in yours. So in these few brief moments, I want to reveal what it means.

First, you have to call upon the two words "I AM." These two words together mean something, so you have to group them and understand that a Human represents the first time they are said, and the second time is a condition, or the meaning is God. Some of you have actually heard the expression, "The great I AM." It is a phrase that means the greatness of God. [It is the personal name of God of the Old Testament (Exodus 3:13-14).] It is the grandness of Spirit, and this concept, when it was first presented, was new. Follow the logic and listen.

If the name of God is, "I AM," then it means that God has a personality, a face, to you, not just a grand detached deity – some power in the sky that has created the planet and the Humans, and that doesn't care. The concept of the I AM would then be a Creator who has sentience, a Creator who has personality, a Creator who can say, "I AM." So then, what comes with it? Love. It is understated; it is invisible; it is understood that the I AM, the great I AM, is the God of love.

Now, if a Human Being said, I AM THAT I AM, the Human Being would seem to be inappropriate, for the Human would be saying, I AM GOD. But you can actually say this in all appropriateness, and mean it in a non-egotistic way. Back to the beginning part of this message: The Human saying: "I am..." then defines what the Human is, spiritually, as the "I AM." So it's really the Human saying. *"I am a Human, and I am part of God."*

As you look around you, there is the observation of God's handiwork everywhere – in the trees, the wind, and you. You are made of the elements of the Earth, which was made by God. You are your own creation, according to almost every Master who walked this planet, who told you: *"There is a piece of the divine inside you."* The very idea of basic duality is a combination of that which is Human, versus that which is God. Every Human has duality. If you have duality, there must be two sides, and one of them is God, in you.

That's the explanation. So when you hear I AM THAT I AM, the statement is easy to understand and very clear. "I am part of the Creative Source, a piece of God." So I ask you again, *"Who are you?"* Do you have this claim? Can you really sit there and say this phrase? I know who's here. I know what you have brought to this place. Let's get personal for a moment. If you are a piece of the Creative Source, then there is no barrier between us. I know what you've been through, and I know why some of you are sitting here. I know these things, because I have been with you, because I'm also a part of God. Your consciousness is part of the consciousness that is connected to Spirit. I have been there during your joys and your tears. We are all the I AM.

Now I ask you, who are you, really? As you sit there, who are you? Can you say and mean it, with pride and belief? I AM THAT I AM! And if you can, say it now.

Indeed.

And so it is.

The Letter N (NEW EARTH, NEW HUMAN)

Given at Mitzpe Shalom (Peace Lookout, Golan Heights) – Saturday morning (Shabbat, the Jewish Sabbath), October 3, 2015

Greetings, dear ones, I am Kryon of Magnetic Service. I know where I am and in a moment we'll tell everyone where we are. The letter that we are going to discuss today is the letter "N." It's going to stand for "NEW EARTH, NEW HUMAN."

Let me explain something to those who are not here. Again, some of the things that I may say will not seem to be appropriate in some ways, for you don't hear some of these things often from spiritual channellings. I feature a practical approach to spirituality, since love is that way.

Human Beings cannot live in the past, spiritually. If God is really God, then God is alive as the Creator, as the I AM, not the I WAS! The I AM means a present God, not a past one. It represents a God with current, beautiful, loving information. It is not a God that is in a book from thousands of years ago. Dear one, history is in a book! God is alive in you! We sit on the Golan Heights. This is an important place for Israel, for so many reasons. But if you are one who deals in military strategy, it is so obvious why it's important now. From where you now sit, high up, overlooking the sea [of Galilee], you could see your enemies coming. This is what I want to speak of.

For years and years and years, groups have been coming to Israel. The biggest industry in Israel is touring. Tens of thousands will come and go from all over the planet. Many want to see and enjoy the history, and then leave. They take their pictures home, along with the memories of a trip. Others will come for spiritual reasons in a group of believers. It will be an emotional experience they will never forget within their own belief system, and they will take it home in their hearts. They will remember that time when they came to either visit the land of Abraham, or the land of Jesus. Others will come, simply because they're interested in history. And then there are those who would come, like you. You have the attribute and belief that your presence here will have an impact, somehow, on the consciousness of the land and the future. Somehow, esoterically, you are planting the seeds for peace, which has not been here in this new energy.

So, practically, let's look at this situation. Let's talk to an Israeli, a wise, practical Israeli, who has been born here, grew up here, and knows about what is here. This Israeli will see the groups come and go, and perhaps work with the tours. He will even see this different group you are in, that claims to be one of consciousness change. But when you leave, this Israeli will roll his eyes and talk among his friends, and he and his friends will say, "Things will never change."

This is not a judgment of this Israeli. It's real, it's practical, and it's because things really never have changed. Generation after generation after generation, they haven't changed. Nobody really gets along with anyone else in this land. Even when Moses was walking in the desert, you had the twelve tribes. Did you know they didn't get along? It even starts earlier than that. Today you have a state [country]. If you haven't been here, you might not understand, but it's not really a country; but rather, it's a state of mind. It's a survival camp still surrounded by ancient enemies, and with a history that was always troublesome.

Israelis are not all Jewish. There are arguments about who owns the land, and who should be here. Jews and non-Jews are all in one place, calling themselves Israelis, even within the Jewish community. There are so many belief systems, that the citizens here walk around each other, carefully. Some are honoring, and some are not. They still don't like each other. This is understandable, if you look at the cauldron of frustration that builds and builds and builds. An Israeli is cynical, and rightfully so. Israelis will look at you, at your consciousness, at your beauty inside, and like it. *"The channellings are lovely and peaceful,"* they will say. Then when you leave, they simply will say, *"Nothing ever will change here. Even while the group is here now, there is violence in Jerusalem."*

You have to understand why this attitude is the case. A westerner will look upon the land with a different perception. They will have a scenario of why things work or don't work, which has nothing to do with the way things really are here. The Golan Heights is where many wars have taken place, even one of them a little more than 40 years ago. So there are many Israelis who will say, *"It's only a matter of time and there will be another and another and another."* It is a way of life, a paradigm for the land, and those who will come and go and visit for whatever reason, are simply tourists.

Now, dear ones, I want to turn the page for a moment. This is important.

For twenty-six years, I have told you about a changing energy, which we will talk about later today. For twenty-six years, we have given you information that this is an important place, and that something will happen here. Most Israelis, even those who would read Kryon, will roll their eyes and they will say, *"It's always going to be the same."*

I would like to enter into a discussion that is metaphoric. We have given you these kinds of examples before, and will again. To the Israelis, I will say this: "The only things you have, in order to have an opinion about your future and your process, is what you have seen in the past. You don't know what you don't know." And perhaps there's something coming that you have never seen before, ever. So because this is not anything that has presented itself in the past, it is not anything that you would think of. It's simply not in your brain to examine as a possibility.

Think for a moment: A man has a disease. He has had it since birth. His father had it before him, and that man's father before him. It comes seemingly with his genealogy, and it's his life. It's in his blood, and the disease is always there. He manages the disease carefully. He watches what he eats, where he goes, and what he says. He knows that the disease can flare up at any time. When it does, he is in survival mode and he beats it up and he wins, and he keeps on going. In his fifties, if you interview this man and say, *"Did you know there is a cure for your disease?"* – he will roll his eyes and say, *"I've heard it before. Not for the past thousand years was there anything. I live with this, and it is me. I know how to handle it. Go away. Get away from me with all of your loving thoughts and your strange cures."* He doesn't know what's coming. He's stuck in a reality that says, "always was, and always will be."

Then a new energy appears on the planet. New technology and new thought starts to come on the scene slowly, and the cure appears. The man is then able to look at it and make up his mind. *"Is it real or should I stay the same? Am I comfortable with my disease?"* Around him, slowly, he sees others with his disease becoming cured, one at a time. Yet, he will not take the cure, because his mindset is one of history. You know what the metaphor is about.

Not too long ago, in another country, we gave you a practical parable: It was about a planet that had a civilization where the people had no eyes. It was normal for them, and as the story went, they got used to it and did well. When one of them was suddenly born with eyes and sight, he got mixed reactions. Some were amazed and understood something new was happening, and some wanted to kill that person, since they felt he was possessed with strange new powers.

So I'll ask you this question yet again: if you have a sightless person in front of you, and they've been sightless since birth, I challenge you to sit with them and explain COLOR. Think on this for a moment. They don't know what they don't know. They don't even have light! How could they understand the spectrum of color? If somehow they gained sight, then they would see and understand color. Do you understand why you meet with such resistance?

I say again to the Earth, to Israel, and to the Israelis: You don't know what you don't know.

Color is coming.

And so it is.

The Letter I (INTO THE FUTURE)

Given in Nimrod Fortress (Mount Hermon)
– Saturday afternoon, October 3, 2015

Greetings, dear ones, I am Kryon of Magnetic Service. Once again, my partner steps away. If you have not heard this phrase before, it is the description of his kind of channelling: He's here, but he's not participating. This is not an out-of-body experience for him, for he's still here. He knows what is being said, using his consciousness, his culture, and his language. He remembers it all. This is the agreement we have had from the beginning. It is not a take-over. Instead, it is a beautiful meld that he has achieved between that which is his Higher-Self and the Human-self. I come in through that portal called the pineal – through the window of his soul – and I use his Higher-Self as a conduit to channel.

For those who are not here and listening (and reading), we are on Mount Hermon, not too far from the Golan Heights in Israel. Mount Hermon is the highest mountain and it allows a view into Lebanon and Syria. Not too far from here is that which I predicted on this planet: There is a dark army without borders, and not even a common language, within view. It is right on schedule, as predicted for this time on the planet, and it will be defeated. [Explosions from Russian bombs in Syria can be heard in the distance, during the channelling.]

We wish to examine the letter "I". This will complete the middle of three words on this channelling journey within Israel. The letter "I" is chosen to stand for "INTO THE FUTURE." This is then an extension or a continuation of the last channel.

We speak about the future of the planet, the future of Israel, and the future of all of you. We talk about things like "wild cards," which is a metaphor for "planned synchronicity." We have used the terminology before. Again we say to you, "You don't know what you don't know." In other words, if you have not seen it yet, you cannot easily conceive it. Futurists try to do this, and those who are specialists in deciding what might be happening next, will do their best as well. Some, with second sight, will also try to move into that future place that no one knows about ... and then they will look around and report. Dear ones, they have all been repeatedly wrong! The reason is because they cannot know what they have never seen or conceptualized.

We talk about wild cards happening on the planet. A wild card is extreme synchronicity that changes places, people, and the planet in ways that no one could conceive of. A real wild card would be outside of the perception of those who would tell the future. In other words, it would never be expected or even thought of as reality. There are several kinds of wild cards, and you have experienced many already. Let me give you some examples.

In the history of the planet, the electricity that you use today came from one man. Now listen to this, for it is the crux of the entire channelling: The invention of alternating current, which is the kind of electricity being used currently, did not come from a committee of scientists. It did not come from a university science group who studied electricity. There were no committees, who were smarter than all other humanity, that put this together. Instead, one man came to this planet with an Akashic purpose. He had a soul that was put here just for that, at the right time and the right place. He was even limited by how much he could do, and was frustrated that he couldn't proceed with what else he had discovered and developed. He died unfulfilled. Nikola Tesla arrived on time, and that was a wild card.

You can tell wild cards because they are not created from multiple consciousness (groups of Humans). They usually stand totally alone. They present themselves normally as singular Humans, in an unexpected event. Sometimes it's one man, one woman, or an extraordinary leader with wise ideas. Sometimes it's an inventor, often an artist or poet, and other times it's a master musician. They make their mark so strongly and so completely, that the world remembers them forever. That is a wild card. You may think it's just normal luck of genealogy? That's funny.

The Chinese have been watching birds and making flying kites for thousands of years. Yet only a hundred years ago, two brothers who made bicycles gave you powered flight. Don't you find that odd? A university or a group of scientists studying the problems of flight, did not create what you see today in your modern air travel. No. Two brothers with an Akashic purpose came to this planet at the right time and opened the knowledge that would give you what you have today. Are you starting to get the picture? Now, if you study their story, they were frustrated, too. They didn't go much further than the pure idea. There was much more to make their discovery elegant, but it was not for them to do. One of them even died early, due to his anxiety over what took place.

Most of you in this room carry an electronic device you've called a smartphone, created by the consciousness of one man at the right time and the right place. You had telephones, and you had portable devices for years. Why didn't a committee put this together? Why didn't a collective intelligence realize the potential? ONE person put together what the brightest minds never thought of: A paradigm shift that changed everything in the way you communicate, and purchase and listen to music. It was a wild card, and the man named Jobs did it with an Akash that came for that – at the right time at the right place, and it changed this planet forever. Why did he have to die so early? Because the planet was not ready for what else he had. He had fulfilled his soul's purpose.

That's a wild card. You experienced a big one in the late '80s. Against all odds, politically, the Soviet Union fell. It disarmed the potential of a World War. Either side disarming would have created that potential. If you are going to have a championship game between two excellent players, and one dies, there's no more game! That's synchronicity. If you ask historians if they expected this event, they would have said, *"Never, never!"* It was a wild card. Have there been other wild cards, perhaps within the history of Israel? Many! Let me give you one that maybe you haven't thought of, and I give it to you as an example while in this land.

Those of you who have been born Jewish have experienced wild cards in your society. So what keeps you from thinking there could be more? There have been many! Let's go back to one that is profound. Every Israeli who is born here at some point is given the story of the Exodus. This beautiful story from slavery to the Promised Land has one man responsible: Moses. What do you think about him? Let's examine this for a moment. Let's examine something that most Israelis are never told much about: What was it like in Egypt before Moses? Was he the only one to ever lead a rebellion of the Jewish slaves? An entire society was enslaved! Do you really think they just sat there and did nothing and endured it until Moses came? And the answer is no. There were many rebellions. It was tried repeatedly, yet nothing worked. The Egyptians were strong. They would kill multiple people, and multiple Jews on a regular basis. They would have everyone watch in order to suppress any kind of rebellion. How much did you study a time before Moses? Not much. I tell you this because there was a large history before Moses.

What are the odds that the Jew who would take you into the Promised Land, would be thought to be Egyptian royalty? This is synchronicity at its best, and a valid wild card. Look at the story and look at how it worked. He had an Akash that was Moses. He was the one who was meant to do it, and who made all the difference in the history for the Jews. Dear ones, it wasn't an accident! It was planned!

Why would you doubt that such a thing might happen again? Why doubt that there would be leadership, not just here, but from other places in the world that would come together in what we would call a confluence of synchronicity that might change this planet forever? Who told you that your miraculous lineage ended centuries ago? It's happened many times, Israeli, to you. So we say yet again in this closing: If you don't know what you don't know, don't prejudge what's going to happen with your doubting energies. Think about it.

And so it is.

———

The Letter E (EXODUS)

Given in the Ancient City of Megiddo (Valley of Armageddon) – Sunday morning, October 4, 2015

Greetings, dear ones, I am Kryon of Magnetic Service. You know where you are and so do I. For those listening (and reading) and are not here, we're in Megiddo. Now that may mean nothing to those not in attendance, but I'll explain in a moment the other name it has.

Some of you have figured it out. We're spelling three words, one letter at a time through thirteen channels. We often do this. It's the "Theme of the Area." You've figured out the three words. "PEACE IN ISRAEL." But it may have been difficult at first, for the spelling was not what you expected. It was spelled for you westerners, backwards. We did it one letter at a time in the English language, but backwards to a western alphabet. The first alphabets, including the ones used here even today that are Arabic and Hebrew, are read and written right to left, so we have chosen to give you these letters in this way to honor the languages of the land. So it is English, written in the Hebrew and Arabic method. The letter that we are going to give you today is one you now expect. It is the final letter of the first word. It's the letter "E." I'll tell you what it means in a moment.

This place has another name. It is the place of Armageddon – apocalypse. I want to review with you what that means. From all of the channels that I have given in this land, this may be the most important. It's important for you; it's important for humanity; it's really important for Israel. This place is where it all was going to end. It is profoundly in Jewish history and prophesies. These lands are to be where the final battles of the planet are fought – the ones to be fought where you sit and would be the Armageddon. It is in Christian prophesy too: These are the final battles. The concept is all over the planet! Wherever you look you find the word Armageddon, and it refers to where you actually sit today. It's almost like the area has been prepared for this – prepared for doom and horror! The people who live around it know it, too. It is in the place in the middle of upper Israel where many battles have already taken place over and over, almost like the land is hardened for the final one. The letter "E" is going to stand for "EXODUS." It is not the exodus that you think. We're going to call this channel, "E – The Second Exodus." The exodus I speak of is one of humanity's future, and consciousness shift.

Now I speak to three hundred of you, and many are sensitives here. Some of you have already felt the energy of the places you've been. It happened in Masada. It happened to some in the river (Jordan), and to some of you in the Sea of Galilee. I want you to be aware of what's here, and I want to be careful, as I talk to you about it. Listen to and read this entire channel, please; don't stop here.

This place represents humanity's duality. It represents the choice to destroy yourselves, and it has always been part of the future of the Human race. You have almost done it four other times! This is not known history, but unknown history. As much as you think you know about history, there was much history before this history. But, dear ones, this was supposed to be the last chance – and immediately the prophecies began.

The Armageddon would happen here. Now, it starts to make sense that it would, and I'm going to tell you why in a moment. But first, the energy: Can you imagine what it's like here, when humanity has had prophecy regarding this place for many generations and feared it? They feared the end, and the prophecy kept coming and the prophets kept talking about it. It became scriptural and many expected it. What happens when layers and layers of fear are projected to one spot? If you are an energy worker here, now you know why you're feeling what you're feeling. It may be inappropriate to say, *"This is not a good place to be."* You're going to leave soon, but you may feel it while you're here. It is the crux of duality, the end of humanity, death on a scale you have never seen.

In my partner's lifetime the prophecies began to come to a focus, with weapons of mass destruction being available to many. Two super-powers on the planet were starting to align themselves for the battle – Armageddon. This is 3D history. This is not esoteric at all. Up to 50,000 nuclear weapons were all pointed at each other not long ago, and the Earth was poised and ready for the Armageddon. Now, that was the prophecy, and now you know why it makes sense that the name of this place corresponds with the prophecy. For the point of contention, that would be the spark of the final world war, would be problems in Israel. This is what would start it. Treaty obligations with Israel would bring in the United States. These would be at odds with treaty obligations of the Soviets. You know how this goes – you drop one, you drop all. War is this way, and always has been. It's very difficult to have a limited-scale war, when you believe you have the means to win it instantly. It's either war or it isn't. It's either life or it's death, and dear ones, you're sitting in death. Please don't turn off the channel. Don't stop listening and reading. But do you see how this made sense? Problems in Israel would create the final war, and this is ground zero. Or is it?

The teaching of the ancient and current indigenous of the planet, as well as that of Kryon, is that the precession of the equinoxes marked a demarcation point to all of humanity. It represents a point of change – one that the planet had never seen before. Human nature was going to start growing up and evolving. Wisdom would begin to be more common. Solutions to hatred would start to occur that you never thought possible. These are not just Kryon's words. These come from the indigenous of the planet, those who have been around for thousands of years before Abraham. That is original prophecy. Here is the overall prophecy of the Ancients: If humanity would make it past 2012, there would be an exodus of old energy. The exodus would be from an old prophecy to a new future, and a new prophecy.

It represents another kind of slavery … coming out of an old land of the slavery of thought, where war seemed to be the only way. Humans would eventually come into a new Promised Land of consciousness, a new, evolved Human nature, where war would eventually be seen as archaic, ugly and never the answer!

Finally, the wisdom of the planet would understand that war begets war, and that it's a disease, and never a solution. Dear ones, if any war on this planet had been a solution, you wouldn't have any more war, and you do, right now.

You are slowly moving into the Promised Land of new thought. When you get up from this place and you leave it, I want you to look back for a moment and understand, it's not what you think anymore. You might even bless it and think about The Exodus. For this place will slowly lose its energy of doom. It will not be the end of anything. It will dissipate eventually, but dear ones, there is something going on that is bigger than any kind of prophecy. If you recognize this, then you're really listening. If you understand what I'm really telling you in this place, you will do something we call cognizing. You'll believe it, and every cell of your body can stand tall and say, *"Now I know why I was born in this time!"* You are Masters, all. You have the wisdom of love, and the solution. The Second Exodus.

Get up from this place differently than you sat down. Say goodbye to the Armageddon as you leave.

And so it is.

The Letter C (COMPASSION)

Given in the Ancient City of Zippori (or Sepphoris) – Sunday afternoon, October 4, 2015

Greetings, dear ones, I am Kryon of Magnetic Service. I come again with another letter! [Laughter] You know by now, what it's going to be. In the English alphabet, it is the letter "C." I'm going to tell you what it represents in just a moment. We're going to talk about consciousness shift very briefly, and in a way that, perhaps, we never have before. I will show you that this planet is actually designed to shift consciousness. It has happened before, dear ones. You are not the first.

We sit upon a place where we can talk about these kinds of things, and it's literally relevant to the dirt that you sit on. I would like to talk to you about your relationship with God. There are those who feel that Human nature never changes, and yet it has. It has changed in history so profoundly, that you restarted your clock! The prophets that you have studied so far, mostly belong to what we have called the God of Law. In fact, the biblical scholars would call it the old testament of humanity – "The Dispensation of Law." Then, two thousand years ago, right in this land, was brought the Jewish prophet, Christ. He gave you a new concept. He was here with an Akash, yes, an Akash (since he was Human), and he was Jewish! Right time, right place – and he changed so much for the entire planet. He changed the perception of the relationship to God. Scripture became new scripture – The New Testament – the new humanity. The One God became the One Loving God. It was an evolvement of thought. Then it became what biblical scholars call "The Dispensation of Love."

Muhammad continued this, and as being the most recent prophet, if you look at that which was spoken so many times, he refers to the love of God, constantly. It's in expression after expression after expression, describing the infinite love of God. You passed from Law to Love, and all the prophets felt it.

Now, in the process of this shift, it was so profound, that you now actually measure time differently! Before Christ (B.C.), and After Christ (A.D.). Do you see what you have done? There was recognition of a consciousness shift! It was so profoundly new, that you had to restart the clock, and the entire planet now measures history with this system. Now, did God change? No. So what changed in this story? Humans did! You did! All of your Akashic records, and all your past lives tell of a Human perception shift from a God of Law, to a God of Love. The letter "C" represents the "DISPENSATION OF COMPASSION."

Did you know that most Israelis have no idea what the Mayan calendar is? There is so much prophecy and so much history here, that it becomes all they really know. There's enough here to fill up their quest for spirituality. But the truth is, there is planetary prophecy as well as Jewish prophecy, and if you knew what the Maya said, you would understand about this dispensation of compassion.

The Maya (and others) created a calendar, a long one of over 5,000 years, but the calendar stopped in 2012. A new calendar was created years ago to start up, if humanity passed December 2012 (at the start of a new cycle of the Precession of the Equinoxes). According to the Mayan calendar prophecy, if humanity would make it past that point without destroying itself, there would be no Armageddon. You would also have to reset the clock again. The clock is one of Human consciousness.

The Dispensation of Compassion is now upon you. It represents compassion for one another. It's wisdom that has not really been seen yet. We speak of this, and speak of this, and speak of this. Yet, some will always say that it is simply esoteric talk. But dear ones, I want you to look at the Ancients and what they did with their clocks. This is not new. Let this be proof that what we are talking about and have spoken of for twenty-five years is not just the words of Kryon. It represents the wisdom of Human ancestors who have reset their clocks when consciousness changed on the planet. It is a precedent!

We say it again: Get ready for new thought. It's more now than just love. It's a mature love that creates compassion for life and humanity. Before I finish, many will ask, *"Who is the next prophet?"* Humans are starting to become mature and wise. What if I told you that in this new energy, the prophet is now within you? Your Higher-Self knows it all! This is the prophet you are now following. This is the new wisdom – the compassion of the Higher-Self.

Where do you sit with this information? How does it feel to you? Let the truth of this be seen in how you see others. Let the truth of your belief in this be seen in how you treat one another. So I say again, as I did in the first channel: "Can you see God in everyone, no matter what?" This is the compassion test.

And so it is.

The Letter A (ASCENSION)

Given on the Summit of Mount Carmel – Monday, October 5, 2015

Greetings, dear ones, I am Kryon of Magnetic Service. Have you felt it yet? Have you, indeed, felt the profundity of this adventure? Here we are in just another tourist area, right? You're going to remember this time.

There are energies here, which may not be repeated like this again. It's a unique group of souls who gather to celebrate this leap with joy, and dance and ponder the history here, and to plant the seeds of new consciousness. This is Elijah country and you know it, and you have been taught it. We've already discussed Elijah and Elisha and the things we wanted you to know about that ascending event.

The letter is "A" and it's right in the middle of the word Peace. We have chosen that letter, and you would think it would then represent the word ascension – not exactly. We're going to call this channel "ASCENSION OF PLANET EARTH," and where better to give this message than the example of ascension and the energy of ascension that is in this region, which is celebrated by so many? There are two parts to this message and I want to be clear on something: Some of this may seem to be a review to those who have followed the words of Kryon for years, and who know why I'm here. They have invested their energy in the concept of an ascending planet, but dear ones, there are so many who have not heard the story. They don't know what I'm going to say, especially those who are from the region. Many are listening (and later reading), and these thirteen channels will eventually be called the Israel Channels. They will be put together as a package of thirteen, and I'm telling my partner right now that they are to be published in many languages. Not all of you know what has been said before. Some of the information is old to many, but revolutionary to many more who have never heard this.

When we say ascension, and we use it in the context of an ascending planet, it doesn't necessarily mean the population of the planet is going to ascend in 3D. We're talking about something different. The best we can describe this in 3D is the ascending vibration of consciousness on Earth. Even that is a metaphor. If you were able to measure Human consciousness on a scale of one to ten, and the ten is mastery, you're in a three at the moment. But dear ones, you've been in three before. You've never really moved much from three. Indeed, you have had concepts of four and five and above, given to you from the Ascended Masters, but you haven't owned it. You haven't lived it, and you're stuck in three.

There is every indication that I'm right, for if you look at humanity, you haven't learned anything. You haven't learned even the basics of getting along. War is not a solution, and as we've said before, hatred begets hatred. It creates it, not solves it. War creates war. Anyone in the process of warring for any reason is going to create more war. That should be obvious from Human history. All you have done is conquer, re-conquer, and conquer again and again. The last two times you were at it, it involved the entire Earth. In fact, the second time was just an extension of the first time ... part II. And (no surprise) it was scheduled yet again ... part III. I want you to think for a moment with me. Would you not agree that the Human nature, which has created this cycle, is not a very wise one? It is immature, and it hasn't figured out the basics of love or compassion. In fact, it hasn't really figured out anything. That's what we're talking about.

Human nature seems to have been the same throughout history, and if you are a psychologist, you are convinced of this. It is simply the way Humans think. This is the premise that you work from, as you help another Human. Human nature is seen as a static, unchanging consciousness of humanity. So it is no wonder that you wring your hands in frustration, for this is all you have ever seen.

There is a metaphor of this, which every parent will understand. When children grow up, they grow through consciousness shift. When they're six to eight years old, there's a certain consciousness that they have. They are socially dysfunctional and immature. They haven't figured out yet what works with other children, or the parents. They're consumed with themselves, since they're just growing up. They're in survival mode, and they have tremendous egos or they have self-worth issues. Very few six to eight year olds are wise and balanced. That comes later. When they get together in the playgrounds of schools, there is peer pressure; they don't understand each other; and sometimes they will assemble themselves in gender specific groups, beliefs, even neighborhoods. They'll throw rocks at one another sometimes, and they may even be the bully of the playground. It's a tough time, and they may even get in a fight or two. They'll go home crying and their parents will be concerned.

This is simple Human development. It has been common throughout history, and then they grow up to become young adults. When they're seventeen or eighteen, they suddenly have elegance; they have learned a wisdom: They have discovered that others their age are similar to themselves and fun to be with. They can have fun, go out together, and enjoy music together like never before. It doesn't matter where they were born or what neighborhood they live in. A seventeen or eighteen year old is not like a six or seven year old. Is this too simple for you? Humanity is stuck in the playground! There's proof. Just look around you. Look at what is happening on the planet now, even still, even today.

An ascending planet is a vibration of consciousness that is starting to climb out of the playground, so that humanity starts to have a wiser Human nature. I am making this very simple for those who have never heard this concept. When we talk about what has happened on the planet, which I'm going to in a moment, this will add credibility to what I'm talking about. Is it possible that you're going to see Human nature evolve? Evolve past what it has been, into an area you have never ever seen? No? You've been told about it. The Masters who walked right here, told you about it.

Turn the page [another subject]. I want to talk about history. I want to give you some information that not all have heard: In certain parts of the world this is so well known, but here, not so much. In this region, you are consumed with the history of the region. You are consumed with the prophets that you have known in the region, and nothing much more. You may not be aware of what I'm going to tell you. There's a bigger picture and I want you to assimilate it and understand it. I want you to go research it. I want you to check it out, because it did not come from Kryon. I'm going to give you a history and prophecy that you may never have heard.

When we were in Istanbul, we gave a channelling called "The Unknown History of the Earth." We did it there, because in that area, and nearby there, there are many new discoveries about places historians cannot understand, with seeming cultures that should not have existed, in languages that they have never seen [cuneiform].

There is much older history than what you think. Even in this region, there is older history than you think. We speak of Sumeria (not Samaria). Sumeria is in the Indus Valley. Go find it. It's more than 9,000 years old, and that's just here!

Dear ones, our teaching has indicated that those who have come from what we would call Lemuria, have an Akash on this planet that is over 30,000 years old. Do you believe that? Now, those in this region listening to this message, don't turn off the channel. Give it a chance. There is evidence that humanity has been here far, far longer than you think. It may actually make this area young!

The Aborigine is an ancient indigenous. Now we're going to use the word indigenous again and again. It means original Human Being in an area. Indigenous – the first ones. Most of them don't have a country. Rather, they have a family, a tribe, and tribal names that you have not heard, which would represent who they are. The Aborigine has been documented in his land for over 30,000 years. That's because there were no conquerors yet. Australia is an isolated continent, and nothing touched it. There were no battles with outsiders. Can you imagine such a thing? The Australian government, which is modern Australia, has documented this age of its own indigenous peoples. The indigenous have been there for 30,000 years.

Now, that means that the Aborigine had been living in their civilization for fifteen or twenty thousand years when Abraham was born! Do you believe me? I want you to go check it out. I want you to look for yourself, so that you will understand what's coming and what I'm going to tell you. How can you have the Sumerians be the start of civilization less than 9,000 years ago, when there was an entire continent of others who were 20,000 years old when the Sumerians were just getting started? There are prophecies some of you have not heard yet, and they come from the first Human Beings on the planet. This is a prophecy that is collective. Collective means it comes from many places through indigenous tribes who have never met one another.

Only recently on the planet has this been discovered: that the same prophecy, which is over 10,000 years old, is also known by the original indigenous everywhere. As in the Letter C channelling, I ask you again: Have you heard of the Mayan calendar? Many of you have not. Some here would say, *"It's a mysterious thing perhaps, in a pagan culture far, far away."* Let's dispel a rumor: They were not pagan! They believed in the One God, but not like you did in this area. Their One God was the Creative Source, which centered on all living things. It all came from one place and they knew it.

The Mayan calendar wasn't just written by the Maya. Three cultures participated in the same prophecy over eons of time, all in the same area. The Aztecs, the Toltecs, and the Maya. Although they had their prophecy, they were still in the old energy. In their cultures, they had unusual ways of treating their conquered temples. They had their wars and their issues and their battles, but when they came upon the temple of the ones they were conquering, they kept it! They even added onto to it, to make it bigger. Pretty soon, through three or four conquerings, it was enormous. This is a bit different than what happened here, isn't it? Go check it out.

Let me tell you their prophecy again in a more complete manner, and when I'm done telling you their prophecy, dear ones, I want you to realize that it is the same prophecy of the indigenous almost all over the Earth. Listen up, for here is a prophecy that is much, much older than anything in the region. Please listen. Please keep listening. This does not diminish the prophecies you have. It adds to them. It helps you to understand your part in all of this.

The Mayan calendar was a calendar of consciousness, not of dates. It didn't even honor the twelve-month system. It was a complete and totally different system. They had something called the long count. I've mentioned it before. It was a very, very long calendar of over 5,000 years that doesn't correspond with days and months, not even the seasons, not really. It was a calendar of energy, a calendar of consciousness. They were tracking Human nature. If you studied their calendar, their prophetic passages actually corresponded to what happened on Earth over time. They were tracking potential times of peace and war on the planet. You can see this in the way they constructed the calendar. Experts have looked at this and seen the projected sweep of Human consciousness going up and down during brief times of peace before war, and then returning. Believe it or not, their prophecy was literally tuned-in to what was happening here! For they predicted the conquering of South America, and more.

The biggest prophesy of the calendar was the one that the other indigenous also had: It was a big one and it corresponded to the movement of the stars. Now the movement of the stars has always been part of tradition, even in this area. I ask you to remember that the Greeks knew about galactic movement. They did. The precession of the equinoxes aligns to a twenty-six thousand year Earth wobble. It was known by the Greeks, by the Romans, and by the Egyptians, who aligned their pyramids to correspond with it and other stars. I give you this information, so you will understand that it is even part of your culture. You talk about the Master Christ – the Master of love in this area? His arrival was foretold by the stars as well. The three wise men who supposedly, traditionally, came to Bethlehem to participate in the birth of a Messiah – were astrologers! What does that tell you? They were referred to as Three Kings, but they were three Master astrologers. Dear ones, the stars have always been part of prophecy. Back to the Maya.

The Mayan calendar stopped in 2012. It had too, because of the prophecy, the one that everyone knows, who is indigenous and has studied it. All over the world it was seen as the end of time. Many,

many cultures were aware of this calendar's end. In December 21, 2012, there was fear on the planet. The Armageddon did not happen, yet there was still a prophecy that looked ominous and fearful – the end of the world in 2012. But that was not the prophesy at all. The end of the calendar was simply the end of an old time.

Here is the prophecy (again). Now listen: What I'm going to tell you is also a summary and generalization of the prophecy of the indigenous of Earth. These are the ones who were here much earlier than anything that happened here, and it is written clearly in the Mayan calendar. Listen: If the planet would pass this marker of 2012, which is represented by the middle point of the wobble of the Earth – a cycle that is 26,000 years old, it would start the beginning of a new consciousness on the planet, and an evolution of vibration. That is the prophecy. Remember my channellings of a day or so ago? Humanity would go from three to four to five and beyond! Human Beings would begin to think differently, and the ascension of consciousness would begin in of all of you.

Now, if you have really figured it out and have begun to use your spiritual logic, and you understand the Akash and the fact that you have lived before, then you really are ready for this. You have been here a long time, old soul. You know what three feels like, and old souls are ready for four. You know what you're doing.

Many of you have waited for this time, but in this region, have you heard this? Have you really heard this or do you think things are impossible, that there are no changes and no reason for changes? That is why we give you the story. There is planetary hope, but it centers here. That's why we're here, because this is where it's going to be the hardest.

Look to the children. At some level, it's possible that the change here will come through your children, who may not agree with you from one generation to another. They may not assimilate the history of the area like you did, and they may do things that shock you and turn against that which you wish them to believe. They may turn away from an old way. It's going to happen through generations of birth. That's the channel. It's bigger than you think, yet the change is centered here.

Dear ones, if I could give you a prophecy, if I could give you a vision that you would understand here, let me do so: Here is the metaphor I see: I can see construction, I can see things happening with thousands of workers, I can see something being built with joy and with solution, without hatred. In my vision, the constructed area is real. I won't tell you when the construction is done, because you won't like the answer. It's the rebuilding of the third temple. Think on this. It's a New Jerusalem, without hatred or war. It comes from a solution that nobody has ever thought of – trust that you would never allow, and discoveries perhaps, that you never thought you'd receive.

That's enough for now. Ascension is bigger than you think.

And so it is.

The Letter E (ENLIGHTENMENT)

Given at Makhtesh Ramon Crater
– Tuesday mid-day, October 6, 2015

Greetings, dear ones, I am Kryon of Magnetic Service. For those who are not here, we sit in the southern part of Israel in a vast expanse of desert, with a view that is amazing. It's a view that has been here as long as the ages, and humanity. This place has been seen by the Ancients and enjoyed, just as you are doing today.

There are two channellings today, and these two will spell the last two letters of the word Peace. We're going to examine the letter "E" and what it would mean in the context of where we sit today. "E" will stand for "ENLIGHTENMENT" and it may not be exactly what you think. The definition of enlightenment will be given, and I want you to pay attention, for it may not be as you have been told. Are you enlightened? How would you then define your own enlightenment?

In honor of the land, we're going to use some riddles. Perhaps not riddles, as much as metaphors or allegories. We're going to ask a fundamental orthodox Jew, "Are you enlightened?" Here would be his answer:

"I am enlightened, more than anybody in the land. For I follow the original laws to the letter. There are no better laws that are closer to God than the ones given here. Our traditions are clear and I, and the rest of us, are doing our best. I am Jewish, I am an enlightened Human Being."

Now, if you ask him about those around him who do not believe as he does, he would say, *"They are not enlightened, for they do not have the truth that I have, and do not follow the rules clearly laid out for us by God and by our ancestors."*

If you ask a Muslim, *"Are you enlightened?"* The man will say:

"Absolutely! I have the original information from the original history of the area, all the way back to Ishmael. But I also have, from this area, a prophet who is more current. Less than a thousand years old, my prophet has the most enlightened information to give to me, as a modern enlightened man. I follow the prophet's words to the letter. How can it get better than that? I have the most modern information."

When you ask him about the others, he would say, *"They do not follow in the steps of my prophet. They don't have full enlightenment. If they do not follow the prophet and his sacred words about God, how could they possibly have enlightenment?"*

Who is enlightened here? Which one is correct, and whose truth is real? If you listen to the justification of their enlightenment, it makes sense, and many of them live their truth in a very pure way. Both groups are pleasing God as best they understand. They are following history, and those who guide them are important historic Humans.

Let's talk to an esoteric person, perhaps one of you. *"Are you enlightened?"* And you would say this:

"We in this group are enlightened, for we have found a God inside, without all of the rules and the trappings of the three-dimensional protocols. Our God is real, because the prophet we follow is inside of us, and this is the most modern thing, following the most ancient thing, we can have. Our meditations are profound. We feel God inside. We are enlightened."

If you ask an esoteric person, what about the others? They would say, *"They don't have what we have, and we pray for them, but they don't have what we have. They are steeped in protocol, and that is not honoring the God inside."*

The orthodox will say, *"We pray for them. Here, let us pray for you, so that you could be like us."* The Muslim is also very willing to bless your family and to pray with you also ... so willing to bring you into a loving God's words like they have with their prophet.

Now let's ask a non-religious Israeli on the street. Let's say we're going to talk to a banker, who does not want anything to do with religion or spirituality or anything that you have today. *"Are you enlightened?"*

This man will look at you and smile and say, *"I really am enlightened, because I have common sense not to be like the others. You won't find me wearing strange things and bowing down, or meditating on a rug somewhere, or contemplating my navel. I'm enlightened, because I'm practical and can work without all these unpractical spiritual practices. I'm a banker. I know how to take care of my family and work within the structure of this world today, not yesterday. I'm proud, I am not foolish like the others."*

Who is right here? Which one really has the truth? Now, first we ask this: Are these people who have spoken really telling you what their heart is saying? And the answer is, yes! Of those who believe in the oneness of God, do they feel it inside them? And the answer is, yes! So how are we going to define enlightenment? How would you do it?

I will tell you what the definition is, from the Creator who lives in you. He lives in every one of those Humans who we just interviewed. The love of God is profound for all humanity. A Human who does not believe in God is still loved just as much as the one who is a fundamentalist. Did you know that? The grandeur of the family of Spirit is beautiful, even if you don't see it. Who is enlightened here?

The definition of enlightenment, as Spirit gives it, is this: An enlightened Human Being is one who respects and sees the enlightenment of all. It's the one who can stand and listen to the orthodox and see God inside of him, and see that it's real and it's perfect for him or her. It's the one who can see the Muslim and understand the beauty of what he believes, and who can look at the esoteric person and understand how close they feel to Spirit, and who can look at the banker and see the same. That is enlightenment. An enlightened Human Being is, therefore, one who emulates the pure attributes of God, rather than any system or that of any other Human. This is also the attribute of Spirit, who will look at every single Human Being with no bias and no preset conditions, and only see family.

We're almost at the beginning of the tour, because that's what we said originally, didn't we? We said to you, "No matter what you see in the next few days, look for God inside." This was a hint for the letter E. Where do you stand? Can you do this really … really?

And so it is.

———

The Letter P (PEACE)

Given at Kfar Hanokdim (Bedouin Village in Negev Desert) – Tuesday evening, October 6, 2015

Greetings, dear ones, I am Kryon of Magnetic Service. My partner, I wish you to go slow. Channelling is translation. It appears as thought groups and intuitive packages of logic presented to the three-dimensional Human brain in a way that then translates into logic and speech. I want this channel to be clear.

We study the final letter, and it is "P." It's the final letter, but it's the first one, as well. So it is part of this circle we have spoken of. The circle has no beginning and has no end. The very word Peace is like that. You see it written in the dirt of this land, scrawled on the walls, representing a hope that seems so elusive. What I wish to do is, again, controversial. A couple of channellings ago, I told you about a bigger prophecy on the planet, and now I wish to give you the rest of the story.

The evening is here. Not too far away is the Dead Sea. A breeze blows, and a chill in the desert air is coming. We sit in a profound place, an ancient place, in order for me to give this final message of the Israeli series. You should know that, esoterically, this planet has had a dark and light balance, and of all the energies, you should recognize that dark has always seemed to win. However, you're not alone, and you fought the light/dark battles with us for eons.

Those who have been called Lightworkers, who have awakened to the One God within, have struggled throughout time to have this message heard. Old souls who gather here and are listening and reading this message, no matter what your culture, no matter where you are on the planet, know of what I speak. The planet has had a low energy for centuries and centuries and this is what we taught and what we gave you, regarding the prophecies and the timing of the prophecies of the Ancients of the indigenous. The Mayan calendar, which represents the overview of this prophecy, goes on to say something you should know. That with a higher consciousness comes a light and dark balance, which shifts. Light starts to become greater than darkness. Now this sounds extremely simple, but it's the only way I can give you what I'm going to give you next. Light is going to win, because the balance of dark and light is now different. Many are starting to feel it, but perhaps not here.

I gave a prophecy back in 2012 and before, and hints of the validity of it are everywhere. I told you that when the light started to become greater than the dark, the darkness would react. I told you that there would be an increase in frustration and evil acts and darkness on this planet. Almost like a last-ditch effort, the dark would be pulling out every possible force that it could to fight this last battle. I told you that light would win, but like a screaming child who doesn't get his way, seeing the light approach, the darkness would become strong and frightening. Have you seen any of that, Israeli?

Let me tell you something: There's a very dark army on your border in Syria, and you may not know this, but they would love to come this direction – and they can't. They can't. It's not just the strength of Israel, it's because Israel is untouchable. There is something you should know, and I'm going to give it to you now. There is more to the phrase "The Chosen Ones" than we discussed before. The ones chosen to give the One God to planet Earth did it, but in the Akash of the Israeli Jew is something extremely esoteric, and the practical proof of this is everywhere.

Past 2012, you are also the ones who would be able to bring light to the planet. We told you this. Now I want you to think for a moment. An Akashic purpose like this is known to humanity at a very, very unconscious level. Have you ever wondered, Jew, what is the reasoning behind what you've gone through since you got here? What is the hatred toward your society all about? What is the anti-Semitism about? What would create this? The conquerors would turn their eyes upon you and wipe you out, destroy the temples, or try genocide. There has to be something more here, and I've just told you what it is. Listen: If the dictator had had his way, he would have eliminated you, because he knew at a subconscious level that he could never, ever win the final battles of Earth, as long as there were Jews. Because the Jews have a hidden light, which is going to then create the peace on this Earth. This would never have worked for his plans.

Everywhere you look at those who have tried to eliminate you, you have found darkness, evil, and this is the dark that we speak of today. It continues. It's there on your news right now. Let's get practical: In the Old City [Jerusalem], it continues, because it knows you're going to win. It's mad and it knows you're going to win! Not only do you carry that Akash to bring the planet the One God, but also to bring it the one peace! It's your lineage, and as long as you existed, no one could stop it. Darkness has always been against you. To many hearing this, they will curse at KRYON and say, "Nonsense!" But in the works is compassion for every person within all the borders here.

I have just given you the explanation of centuries of persecution, from an esoteric level. I want you to look at this. Does it make sense to you now? Does it? Then, let me give you a parable. This society loves stories and you have plenty of them.

I want to give you the parable of Wo, the Frustrated Farmer. Wo was a farmer and he knew what he was doing. He had some of the best tools and the best seeds, he thought, to make the finest crops that ever could exist on the planet. He was frustrated, however, because nothing grew! Wo always felt that perhaps he was ahead of his time, because nothing grew. It was worse than that. In his fields, there seemed to be enemies everywhere. Things would hide his seeds, steal his seeds, and kill his seeds. No matter what he did, the crops were just pathetic. He never really got ahold of what he absolutely knew could be there, for years and years and years. Nothing grew.

Many tried to help him. They came with great wise seeds, and he'd plant them, and nothing would happen. He was so frustrated! He knew intuitively that his seeds were connected to the great Central Source, and that if he could just get them going, they would be beautiful. They would change farming forever! Wo had an original set of seeds, and he tried them many times – they didn't work. He abandoned them a long time ago. He tried everything he could. He was frustrated.

Years went by, and then something happened on the planet. Climate changed. More than that, something was in the air. Wo was frustrated, so he didn't figure that it meant anything different for him, but he thought he'd try. He took the original seeds he was given, and planted them in this new condition. As he pushed them into the ground, he felt they went in differently; the ground felt more fertile. Wo actually had some hope. He planted them all. The climate change cooperated, and he started to water them.

Now this is where the parable goes in a different direction than you thought. Nothing happened, and Wo said to himself, *"I knew it!"* Nothing ever changes. Those original seeds didn't work the first time, and they're not going to work this time. Every morning, he would come out and look at the new seeds, and they did nothing. He expected so much, yet they did nothing. Wo eventually passed away, a frustrated man. However, Wo had two sons, and his sons knew better. They felt it. They didn't have the frustration that Wo had. They had an odd renewed hope, and they knew the climate was changing too. But they felt something was happening in history.

The sons would watch the seeds and indeed, like when Wo watched, nothing happened. Finally one day, when things were really starting to shift and change, there came some result! The seeds started to come up, and the sons were quite excited. The next day, these odd seeds started to go back down! This was strange indeed. The next day, they were up again, and the next day, they went down. Finally, over a period of time, the sons realized the seeds were blossoming; they were growing! These were unusual compassion seeds, different than any that ever existed, but they were the originals, and the sons knew that, when the timing was right, they would have the best crop on the planet, and would be able to share it with everyone.

Listen, Israeli, this is your planting field. The crops represent the energy that is here and the Akash that you carry. The frustration has been, that through years, the timing was not right. When Wo planted the new seeds, he did it properly and correctly. He had a new climate and he felt it. He knew it would happen, even though he was not there to see it. What happens when you plant no seeds, Israeli? Are you so frustrated that you have no hope, because the climate is changing? Do you see things apparently sliding backwards, and give up? In this society, there has been so much courage, so much heroism, so much suffering, and so much patience. You've seen it in your prophets over and over.

Don't stop now, just because it never worked before. Now it's time. And if the seniors don't see it, young people – you will. Don't let the dark armies make you afraid. Because you hold the light of what's next.

Listen: Color is coming.

And so it is.

Chapter Ten

Five in a Circle

Not everyone is the same, and Kryon has been giving us messages about our differences for many years. This was the first channelling, however, in which he outlined five different personality types, that all fit into a puzzle. The puzzle? It's why we are so different, and how we actually help each other, through these differences. Do you recognize anyone in this channelled scenario? Do you, perhaps, recognize yourself? The main message here is that we are all in a circle; even though we are vastly different, we support each other in many ways. This channelling was the most recent one given (2016) that is included in this Book 14, and continues to be one of my favorites.

Lee Carroll

Chapter Ten

"Five in a Circle"

Kryon Live Channelling
Given in Phoenix, Arizona

January 16, 2016

G reetings, dear ones, I am Kryon of Magnetic Service. I would like this to be an informative channel, but I want you to relate to it. My partner steps aside so completely, he has no idea what's coming. I've given him an idea of what might be discussed, so it is not a mystery. But other than that, he doesn't know much more.

Dear ones, I want to do something that sometimes is dangerous to your logic. It's dangerous only because your logic often intercedes when it hears new information and gives you false alarms based on your biases. So we ask you to be open for beautiful new ideas.

I don't like to give you lists, because you always make them hierarchical. Number one is more important than number two, etc. Anytime anything is delivered as "one, two, three, four," there is a tendency, with a logical brain, to put one above the other. So let me ask you, what other option do I have than to make a list? I cannot give you everything at once, since you can't receive it that way. That would, indeed, be quantum and desirable, but I must give things to you one by one. I number them so you can feel the energy of the numbers. But your logic will try to make them hierarchical – a linear bias.

I'm going to set this up so it will be more understandable. I want to give you information that helps to identify the beautiful roles of Old Souls and Lightworkers, who are working every day on solutions to solve new-energy puzzles on this planet. In order to do that, I'm going to have to itemize who some of you are, because of your Akash, and what you are doing here. I'll be giving you some names to consider to help identify the types of roles, but I want you to know something first: I'm going to give all this information "in a circle." So the list is really a circle, and not a linear ladder.

Think of a ring for a moment. It's beautiful, together, unbroken, and circular. It doesn't matter on the ring where you start anything, or which direction you go, since you'll get all the attributes and the knowledge, because it all comes back to where it started, or ended. Now, in linearity, in a straight line that you call time, I'm going to give you this information. But no role or name is more or less important than the one before or following. So what I'm about to give you doesn't have any hierarchical meaning at all.

Before we begin, I've just given you information that also applies to one of the most difficult spiritual attributes of the new energy: When Spirit talks to Humans or even one Human, we can only talk to you about one item at a time. Sometimes, you grab the first item and you never listen to number two, three, or four. Your truth then becomes only number one! If you were to open your heart and your mind and listen to all of them, and take them all in, you would realize that truth is bigger than one, and you would be a wiser spiritual person. However, the bias of humanity is that it singularizes one thing at a time, because of your linearity, and then acts only on that idea.

Spiritual systems on your planet normally carry a singular purpose, no matter what that spiritual system is or what you call it. It has you looking at rules and doctrines, and it's up to you to obey them the best you can. The idea is "sameness of purpose" for all those involved in that specific belief. In some systems you would all wear the same thing, act a certain way, meditate at a certain place, pray at a certain time, bow in the same direction, and do it in the same way. This is seen as "honoring God" and is what we call "beginning spiritual survival." It's the way you have been told by your elders, that Humans work with God.

However, if you take a good look at any complex natural system on this planet, or in the galaxy, you will find all parts doing many different things to fit into the same goal. If you look at physics, parts are doing different things, dedicated to different energies, but working within the same system. Look at chemistry: Profoundly, the parts come together, in order to create elegant results, which are greater than the parts. Everywhere you look in nature, you see the same thing: One system supports the other. The very system of life with oxygen and carbon dioxide on your planet is a symbiotic cooperative system that keeps you alive. The fine Swiss clock only can operate if all the various wheels and gears do their job.

What if I told you that suddenly, all of these parts were going to dress the same, and do the same thing, and ignore or fight with the other parts? You'd say, *"That's not going to be a workable solution at all! They need to cooperate! Everything would stop!"* You'd be right. Do you see perhaps, a need to become less linear in these times?

Dear ones, there is a very new, wise energy on this planet, and there is an elegant system in front of you that Old Souls are beginning to see. So let's back up a bit and review: You're here for a reason and for a purpose. Many of you have awakened to a bigger truth – a truth that is so big and so beautiful, that it's like nothing seen before on the Earth. It's a truth that doesn't make anybody else wrong. It's a truth that enhances all humanity, no matter what others believe. The truth is this: God is inside you, and you are all a spiritual family. Another truth: The energy on this planet is shifting, allowing for greater wisdom. Another truth: Those who have repeatedly been born on this planet for eons, carry the greatest wisdom, especially for this time. They are called Old Souls. Another truth: These Old Souls are waking up to different tasks, in order to supply a more elegant solution for this new energy.

The Types of Old Souls – Five in a Circle

So I want to talk about the various slots that you go into – the roles you play in the circle of five. It sounds very linear, and so you may recognize yourself. It's complex, but I'm going to make it simple. So I'm only going to create five slots today.

Now, everything I talk about from now on, will be analyzed by many, later. This is typical of the Kryon work. You will find hidden meanings in most of it, specifically, in the numerology. Dear ones, I give you messages within messages, so that you can study these things later, and see that there's more, much more than what I present in the language of my partner.

Let this be a time for understanding. Not just understanding, but celebration. There are those listening to this and reading later, who need to hear these new truths. Some of you look at the teachers, authors and leaders of this New Age, and feel you are not carrying your weight. However, it's not that way at all. This is only a linear perception, based on an older system of what you think is important or not.

It's easy to understand: You all have different spiritual tasks right now, and the thing that drives them all, and puts you into these roles in the circle that we want to show you, is your Akash. The energy of who you were and what you've done, creates who you are now. It creates your spiritual purpose, and other normal life attributes: What you're interested in, your talents, and your fears. But in this discussion, we're talking about Old Souls and spiritual purpose. We are speaking about what you're doing currently in this shift, and why you're here.

As I mentioned, it is dangerous to categorize Humans in any form, because of the singularity of your bias. You automatically carry it further. You may say, *"Well, I'm in this category or role called this or that, and therefore, I'm not doing enough, since the other categories are more important."* I have to ask you to suspend all of that and just listen. I want to tell you about Old Souls and what they do, and how they work together in a beautiful circle that's golden. It's a circle of love and creation, and the Old Souls and the Lightworkers come into this planet with a perfect solution, and perfect numbers, and create perfect balance – and you never even know there's a system!

Role Number One – Akashic Entanglement

I want to start with my partner and those like him. I'll use terminology I haven't used before: Akashic entanglement. What do you know about the word entanglement? Very little, actually. It is a fairly new word created by your physicists, which basically means a shared reality. If two things are entangled in physics, they both have the same reality, even if they're removed, one from the other, in different places. It's a quantum expression, a shared reality that can even be on different sides of the galaxy.

One who is entangled with their own Akash is sharing the reality of something that pushes them from the past. It's difficult for this person to decipher the reality of that which is Earthly, from the reality of that which is from the Akashic past, or a reality that exists on the other side of the veil. But they are "driven" by their Akashic perceptions.

Now, there's a word used in astrology, and it is a metaphor for this person. The word is YOD – Y - O - D. In astrology, it is an alignment of three things, which are unique and special that don't happen very often. For those born with it, it creates an energy that focuses the individual in a specific (and difficult to understand) way. They live and breathe what they think they need to do, and it comes from their Akash. It doesn't just happen, dear ones, because you're born with these attributes. Like all astrological energies, they posture your potentials, should you awaken into them. In other words, if you choose not to accept these things, they'll never occur for you, but once you start the path of examination, they'll capture you in a good way, and push you so hard, that everything you do is only about one thing. You become an ultra-focused Old Soul for God!

This category of Akashically entangled Old Souls is for those who are constantly pushed to do work. Some are channellers; some are authors; some are writers; some are speakers. Their lives may seem normal, but they are not. All they do in their waking hours is think about why they're here. They'll push themselves constantly with the energy from the Akash, until the day they take their last breath. It is about one singular, focused, pushed thing. It's beautiful, because they get a lot done. But there's a way of thinking from others, which looks at them and says, *"Oh look at that! I should do that. I'm not really doing anything compared to that!"* or *"Look at that! They never have time for anyone or anything but their own work."* So within this discussion, I want to talk about this very biased thinking among Lightworkers.

Dear ones, in the five categories, there must be those who have an entangled Akash, in order to push this new energy into fast-forward, as they do. It has to be. My partner knows this and he's seeing himself change. He now realizes this is all he's going to do. He realizes he's never going to retire. Somehow, that would be a betrayal of his Akash. He's going to push until it's over, and he knows others who are just like him. It's all they want to do. They see the beauty and splendor of the other side of the veil, and all they can do is tell about it, write about it, teach it, and be it.

That's Akashic entanglement. My partner is comfortable with it now, and it's all he wants to do. That's number one. Remember what a one is in numerology? It represents the energy of new beginnings. That is the whole purpose of those who are pushed by their Akashic entanglement. They are so focused by everything they do, everywhere they go, that it all represents a new beginning. They don't end anything, and often don't look backwards to review anything they did. It's never complete. It's always new. Number one.

Role Number Two – Partial Akashic Entanglement

Number two is similar – Partially entangled Akash. These are represented by those who don't have quite the push, but they still feel as though they do. However, they're a little more relaxed with it. It's okay to retire or relax with life, but they always feel they have a solid purpose on the planet.

Now these, number two, deal with duality and 3D. They deal more with the Human body. They are healers and are the ones who are looking for solutions that will support number one. Number one tends to overdo it, and needs number two to heal them!

Partially Akashic entangled individuals are often system workers, and they've got it figured out. They come up with systems that help humanity. Indeed, they are focused too, and they can remember that they've been healers before. They can remember some of the systems that they're working with that they've used before. They are so sure of it, that they want to write about it and teach it. It's so obvious. They steward new systems, and love to put things together.

They are a support group for humanity, and also for number one! Number one would push himself without eating, unless he had somebody to tell him to eat. Number two will develop a system of what to eat! There is a beautiful symbiosis here. Again, it's like a Swiss clock, in which one gear fits into the other. The thing that ties these five together, and I'm telling you even before I give you the rest of them, is synchronicity.

When I'm finished teaching today, I will have given you five types and roles. There is an immediate tendency for you to say, *"Which one am I?"* Well, dear linear one, did I tell you that you could be a combo? Did I tell you there is a crossover? Did I tell you there are gray areas? Did I tell you it's quantum? Don't try to fit yourself into these slots. Just know they exist and you may match one of them completely, or may fit to some degree in several. But understand you're part of the mechanism of this beautiful clock that moves around in your own time and fits together. One fits to the other because they all support one another. Just wait until I tell you about number three.

Role Number Three – The Meditators

The number three is the energy of the catalyst. It moves things. The very existence of role number three is catalytic. A catalyst is something that stays the same, but changes things it comes in contact with. I'll tell you who these are. These are the meditators of the planet! Their Akash is so comfortable doing this, because they can sit and meditate for days and they will come out refreshed. They will often sit in one position for all of it.

What are they really doing? I'll tell you what they're doing: They are holding the energy of all the others together, because their consciousness is steady. Don't confuse this with an anchor, for it's not. It holds harmony. It's quiet and beautiful, and it sets a stage that all the others feel. I want to tell you about this clock and the circle. When number one comes to frustration, number three is part of him. He feels number three, and it satisfies his need to relax. The meditative side is not part of number one at all: Push, push, go! Number three then takes it to another level, in a quantum way, and shares it with number one and number two. Then both of them have peace and they relax, and know all is well – all this because number three is here and doing his/her job. Do you see how this works together?

Number three has had lifetimes of being a monk all over the planet, and has learned to sit and just be. There is so much power here with the quantum meditator! Tell me, as a Lightworker, have you ever looked at number three and said, *"How can you do that? It's not for me. You just sit there – for hours and hours!"* Now you know. They just sit there and steady the planet. They steady and harmonize all of the other numbers, because they absorb them and give them peace. They create a peaceful countenance and whatever comes their way is more peaceful because of it.

Number one and number two need number three desperately, but number three also needs number one and number two. This is because just "sitting there" doesn't accomplish what number one and two can do! Are you starting to understand the circle? Does it make sense to you? Does it make sense that there would be a system where Old Souls do different things for the planet to make it work? They are not all in one uniform, not all of one gender, not all in one doctrine and belief system, not doing the same thing, not singing the same songs, but totally, completely unique and different, and yet, fitting together like a fine Swiss clock.

Role Number Four – The Tree Hugger

What do you think number four is? If you've been numerologically educated, number four is the Gaia number. Have you ever heard me tell you before, that Gaia is related to Human consciousness? The planet Earth is connected to you, profoundly. If you ask the Ancients about this, they will tell you that it's the first thing they absolutely knew about! There was no technology back then. Gaia gave them their food, showed them where to hunt and fish, and gave them good weather when they needed it. All of these things were the most important things they had, and the most spiritual. Gaia was connected to God.

Dear ones, you've lost that, and today that profound connection is not as important to you, but it can be again. Let me tell you about number four: Some of these Humans don't even know they are Lightworkers. They just know they're connected to the Earth. But they're passionately connected to the Earth! You can't pry them off a tree when they're hugging it. They need to be part of Gaia all the time.

Question coming from the audience [which is being intuited]: *"Dear Kryon, about these five: Can someone change one kind, and change to the next kind in one lifetime?"* Humans, why do you do this? You are intellectualizing the minutia of the message, before it's even complete! Yes, you can do whatever you want to, since you may have a very rich Akash. Think about this: Can a number three become a number four? Can a number five, which you haven't even heard of, become a number one? The system is in a circle, so of course you can! There are ways for you to pick up energies, learn things, and move around the circle. It's dynamic and beautiful. Humans think that as soon as something is learned, it gets put into a place and stays there forever. It's like you get in a box and shut the door, then you live with it. Dear ones, you're part of the circle. You move with it.

Number four is also an animal whisperer, an animal lover; someone who can literally speak to that which is the consciousness of animals or understand them. Number four is also one who will talk to the plants and actually feel that the plants have something to say! They love the planet. That's number four.

Now, if you're number three and you're contemplating your navel for three days, you're not really going to understand the gardener who gets up very early and plants things and loves it, just loves it! But if you're in a circle working together, and you're entangled a little, then you're all helping one another, and you all have a piece of your specialty. Did you hear that? It's part of a grand system.

The animal whisperer is whispering for number one and two and three. Yet number three or two or one may not hear or know, but it's happening anyway by default. It needs to, because Human consciousness is connected in quantum ways, not isolated. You think you have one soul doing one thing? My partner showed you today that the confluence of consciousness is what moves things. Not one, not two, not three, but a confluence of many mixed together. I'm telling you there's a circle of workers that help one another because they intermingle their consciousness, but they have specialties. When these specialties are put together, they create balance. Does this remind you of "mother nature"?

This is what a quantum system is like. It's made of many parts that mix with the other parts, yet some of the parts don't know each other, or even understand each other. You get help from those who are meditating, even if you are not a meditator. They become part of you. The whole is stronger than the parts because of this. That was number four.

Oh, there are so many fours. It calls to you. Some Humans never move off the peg of the love of planet Earth, and they don't even call themselves Old Souls. They feel they are just Earth-workers. They don't even know about their Akash. They just know, for some reason, all they want to do is be with nature, and the animals. That's all they want to do, never realizing that it's shared with number three and with number two. The one who is working on systems (number two) is also hugging the tree because of number four. That great Earth peace is generated by number four and is helped greatly by number three, sitting there for hours, still and peaceful for all of them. Number one is still going out and pushing and pushing and pushing. That's in order to change the planet for the rest of them. It's a beautiful system.

Role Number Five – Anchors

Number five is the last one for now. Change is the meaning of the number five. Who is the biggest changer of the planet? Well, some would say it has to be number one. No, it isn't. Number one does his or her job in a way that is so focused and pinpointed, that it will take years to make a difference. Even then, it will be meaningful only to certain people. No, it's number five that makes the biggest difference. Number five has more Old Souls in the group than any other compartment. I'll call them the Anchors. They anchor number one, two, three and four.

If you are number four, what good does it do to hug a tree all your life? Who are you going to talk to? Who are you going to help? The answer is, "All the rest of them." This is because of your relationship to the planet. Do you see how this works? Number five is going to anchor number four, and especially number three, who might float away, without something to hold on to! Number one doesn't even want to stop to smell the roses.

The number fives are the Old Souls who go about their lives without writing a book, without being on stage, and without doing anything "important," as they perceive important. They walk, day by day, not understanding that they are on this planet spreading compassionate action. Compassion the key word, and we've used it over and over. It is that which this planet needs to change, and it anchors balance.

Every day, the Old Soul goes to work, has friends and family, goes to school, and all the other things that life offers. It's really only number five who comes into contact with the others on the planet. But it's how they treat other Humans that is the anchor. How do you act on the freeways of life, Old Soul? Is it compassionate? Do you see God in others? Number five is the one who anchors, and it does more to help this planet than all of the other numbers together. The anchor spreads the compassion that this planet needs, so that all the other numbers can work their specialties.

Who are you? Maybe you are a combination of several, and that's okay, because these categories are really not singular. I put them in five compartments, but now I'm going to tear apart the walls of the compartments and mix number one through five together in a blender. That's quantum. You may not really understands that, dear ones, but at least you now understand there is a beautiful system which honors the differences. That's why there are so many varied interests in spirituality. Some will ask, *"Which one am I? I don't seem to be any of them."* What you do not understand is that you're doing everything! You're supporting all the others, and are probably a number five.

Number five, I want you to listen to this: What you're doing by simply walking this planet in a compassionate way is critical to the system. Without this, numbers one through four won't accomplish anything. Number one can pound the message home to a dispassionate Earth, and it won't matter at all, unless he has support. Number two can have systems and can give them to a dispassionate Earth, and nobody is going to hear it, unless he has support. Number three may sit and ponder everything for years, yet it won't do anything to help an Earth that doesn't care. Number four can hug all the trees he wants to and be connected to Gaia, but unless there is a compassionate Earth, nothing will change. Number five? It seems like I'm saying that he/she is the most important, but not really. Alone, number five can't accomplish much without the rest, either. Number five can help prepare the planet, but like the farmer who prepares the ground, without the seeds, there is no growth. It's back to the fine Swiss clock. What gear is most important?

When you leave this place, think about this: The consciousness of humanity is still wallowing in the old energy. Have you seen the media programs that you are being offered? You can tune in and watch families argue and call each other names! Don't you have enough of that already at home? Now you are offered some more!

Instead, how about programs with compassionate elements? There are wonderful stories of heroism within families, love stories, and beautiful victories. Let the drama be tears of joy and compassion! Would it work? It will someday.

Dear ones, this is the way Old Souls and spiritually-minded Humans work in this new energy. It's a system put together by Old Souls and workers of the light, where everyone plays their own specific roles. It's not where everyone does the same thing, or follows only one rule of truth. This is a confluence of energy that works this puzzle in a beautiful golden circle. You don't all have to wear the same outfit, or face the same direction, or speak the same language, to change the planet. You also don't even have to know each other.

This is just the beginning and there will be more, but the premise is clear: Everyone has their niche, depending upon who they are, and how many lives they have had on the Earth. The Old Souls are the most experienced, and will recognize this message first. This system begins to explain why some of you are called to do certain things, and others are not. Dear ones, don't beat yourselves up mentally, because you don't think you measure up to your neighbor, who you feel is doing something more important than yourself. God sees you all the same, working the puzzle together.

Leave this place differently than you came, with knowledge that is uplifting, and a change of attitude about what might be happening for you. That's enough for today.

I am Kryon, in love with humanity.

And so it is.

NEW!

Messages to Connect with the Energy of the Earth
by Monika Muranyi

This card deck has been carefully designed to help you reconnect with our precious Mother Earth - Gaia. Using extracts from the loving channelled messages of Kryon, the intent is to rekindle the compassionate communication of Gaia's consciousness with you. Full color 44-card Deck with color guidebook.
Beautiful designs by artist Deborah DeLisi

ISBN: 978-1-888053-17-3 $19.95

www.kryon.com

Drop by and visit
KRYON CENTRAL

The award winning Kryon website allows you to find the latest information on seminars schedules, and Kryon related products.Browse through portions of Kryon books, read some of the most profound Kryon channellings, enjoy some of the hundreds of answers in the Kryon Q&A section, and watch free videos.

Kryon's website offers the latest in technology and is easy to navigate. Our main menu allows you a very simple guide to all the main areas of our site. It is formatted specifically for mobile devices too!

www.kryon.com

GET CONNECTED
TO KRYON!

Sign up to receive the welcome edition of our Kryon Family Newsletter. You will receive a monthly edition, plus occasional extra bulletins from Lee, and even the very popular Marshmallow messages. You will receive…

• A personal blog from Lee on current happenings
• The latest Kryon information
• Up-to-date schedule of Lee's events world-wide
• Marshmallow messages - profound Kryon sayings

www.kryon.com/get-connected

GET CONNECTED

www.kryon.com

Kryon Smart Phone Apps

AKASHIC POWER

AFFIRMATIONS FOR YOUR SOUL

Here are the first KRYON smartphone APPS for Apple and Android! Each application allows many channellings and affirmations, with helpful categories that allow you to either get in touch with your Akashic energy, or Affirm your truths through powerful affirmations . **LOOK:** There are 9 audio channellings in AKASHIC POWER and 105 audios in AFFIRMATIONS FOR YOUR SOUL. These applications download to your phone and do not need the Internet to operate once downloaded. You can even design your own affirmations! Consult the Apple and Android stores for purchase.

FIRST EVER
Kryon-Compiled Books!

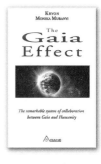  

TITLES:

- **The Gaia Effect** - The remarkable system of collaboration between Gaia and Humanity
  ISBN 978-2-896261-132-1
  2013 - Editions-Ariane - Canada • 300 pages - $16.00 USA

- **The Human Akash** - A Discovery of The Blueprint Within
  ISBN 978-2-89626-173-4
  2014 - Editions-Ariane - Canada • 300 pages - $16.00 USA

- **The Human Soul Revealed** - Unlocking the Mysteries from Beyond
  ISBN 978-2-89626-255-7
  2015 - Editions-Ariane - Canada • 300 pages - $16.00 USA

Author **Monika Muranyi** has taken some of the most profound KRYON channellings, compiled them into these very popular subjects, and has written commentary around all of them. Not only that, but she then asks KRYON many questions to clarify issues given within the channellings! The channellings are from Lee Carroll and KRYON, and the compilations and explanations are from Monika. This is a long overdue trilogy of over 25 years of the KRYON writing into subject-driven books.

LOOK: If you want more - Monika has put additional chapters on her website!
www.monikamuranyi.com

www.kryon.com/store
Also available as ebooks on-line

Kryon Compiled Books!

A PROFOUND DNA ACTIVATION PROCESS
by Jan Tober

JAN TOBER is an International speaker, healer, and facilitator.

She is co-author of the best selling *Indigo Children* series by Hay House books, having introduced the very term Indigo Children along with Lee Carroll in 1999. Co-creator of the Kryon work, she continues to bring her healing voice to thousands.

In recent years, Jan has been able to offer her unique personalized DNA sound activation process, and the international reviews are unanimous and inspiring. Using the crystal bowls from CRYSTAL TONES www.crystalsingingbowls.com, Jan creates a custom CD recording, guided by your personal birth information. This is a DNA activation and ascension process that she has developed over many years, using her healing voice and the renowned quality of the singing crystal bowls... even using a special KRYON BOWL!

Please visit Jan's website for ordering and price information:
[**www.jantober.com**]

Manifesting Your Mastery
44 - Card Deck
by Monika Muranyi

ISBN 978-1-888053-15-9
Publisher **The Kryon Writings** - $19.95 USD

Affirmations are one of the most powerful methods of self-healing for our bodies and minds. Monika Muranyi, author of the special compiled Kryon book trilogy, has carefully created the Manifesting Your Mastery 44-Card Deck.

Inspired by the writings of KRYON, the deck is filled with daily affirmations designed to enhance soul communication and life force. Within this deck are 44 affirmation cards, and a guidebook to help you create your own affirmations, along with suggestions on how to use them.

The affirmations are presented in many categories: health, relationships, business/money, life-pupose, creating peace, and more. The purpose of these affirmations is to help you remember and use your magnificence to enhance your eternal connection with the Creative Source.

Mastery Affirmation Cards

UP CLOSE
WITH KRYON!

Get together for a personal time with
Kryon and Lee Carroll!

Lee now presents in many cities all over the USA and Canada with an all-day seminar featuring the latest information from Kryon. Often presented with a sit-down lunch included, it's the most popular way to join in the Kryon energy.

The special meetings include discussion by Lee Carroll regarding timely New Age topics, and then it continues during the day with profound, inspired teachings from the Kryon work. Kryon channelling occurs at least two times in each meeting. Quite often Lee is also joined by talented speakers and special guests. Group size is typically 100 to 150 people. Often lasting up to five and a half hours, it's an event you won't forget!

Check out [www.kryon.com/schedule] to see if there is an event close to you!

Kryon at the United Nations

Lee Carroll - UN visit 2005

Seven times since 1995, Lee Carroll and Kryon have been invited to lecture and channel at the S.E.A.T. (Society for Enlightenment and Transformation) at the United Nations in New York City. By invitation, he has brought a time of lecture, meditation and channelling to an elite group of U.N. delegates and guests.

Kryon Book Six, Partnering with God, carried the first two entire transcripts of what Kryon had to say... some of which has now been validated by the scientific community. Kryon Book Seven, Letters from Home, carries the meeting in 1998. The 2005 and 2006 transcriptions are in Kryon Book Eleven, Lifting the Veil. All Seven of these transcripts are on the Kryon Website [www.kryon.com/channelling], up through 2009.

Our sincere thanks to Zehra Boccia for her help with introducing us to the presidents of this organization over the years. We thank the S.E.A.T for the invitations, and for their spiritual work, which helps to further enlighten our planet.

Index

Index

Index